Dictionary of Beer

Edited by Anne Webb

CAMRA Dictionary of Beer

Edited by Anne Webb

Cover photography by Tracy Sherwood
Cover design by McKie Associates
Printed by WS Bookwell, Finland

Published by CAMRA, The Campaign for Real Ale, 230 Hatfield Road, St. Albans, Herts AL1 4LW

Managing Editor: Mark Webb, mark-webb@msn. com

© CAMRA Ltd 2001

ISBN 1-85249-158-2

Introduction

The first Dictionary of Beer compiled by CAMRA was published in 1985 and met with general approval. It sold out but the project was never revived. This second CAMRA Dictionary of Beer has been completely revised and updated to provide an invaluable resource for beer enthusiasts, be they real ale drinkers or not, homebrewers, student brewers, publicans – even travellers in Europe, who could use this publication as a phrase book to understanding their beer labels abroad. At the very least, this book offers players of Scrabble and Countdown an intoxicating collection of beer mots to draw upon.

Using this dictionary

The CAMRA Dictionary of Beer provides extensive coverage of general, specific, scientific, historical, up-to-date, political, foreign and linguistic words and phrases.

Each entry is highlighted in bold style and defined clearly, with examples, chemical formulae, abbreviations, cross references, and subjective comments etc. where applicable. Specific categories are indicated in italics in brackets. Abbreviations and acronyms are also listed as separate entries. Some international beers have been selected for entry. British Isles breweries and some international concerns are also listed.

Pronunciation guides have been omitted, as the foreign entries are given solely as a reference to understanding beer labels abroad. For ease of use the foreign characters have been entered alphabetically following the standard English alphabet e.g. épices is listed after enzyme and before Epsom salts. Abbreviations indicating the status of a word (whether it is a noun, adjective etc.) have not been given, although if it is a verb, (to) is highlighted in bold after the entry e.g. kräusen (to).

More words

The CAMRA Dictionary of Beer is a serious endeavour to catalogue the language of beer and brewing and the editors at CAMRA welcome any contributions for a future edition, either concerning the words in the Dictionary or new words for us to add. The international scope of the Dictionary means that there are inevitably many more words (and their definitions) out there which we don't know about. Send them in to us at CAMRA, 230 Hatfield Road, St Albans, Herts, AL1 4LW, UK. You can email them to:

Anne.Webb@tesco.net

Contributors and advisors

Brewing entries revised by:
DAL, Technical Brewing Consultants, Tel: +44 (0) 1536 511715
enquiries@dal.eu.com
www.dal.eu.com
Beer evaluation entries approved by:
Dr. Keith Thomas, BREWLAB, University of Sunderland, SR1 3SD
Tel: +44 (0)191 515 2535
www.brewlab.co.uk

Foreign language entries approved by:
Eva Bartasius
Eva Jungfalk Down
Marta Mase
Martina Muselikova

Slang terms offered by:
Mike Cummins

Thanks also to:
Brian Glover, editor of the original CAMRA Dictionary of Beer
Iain Loe for content ideas

Bibliography

Bier brauen, Handbuch für den Heimbrauer, Richard Lehrl, 2000 Verlag Eugen Ulmer GmbH & Co.

Bier aus eigenem Keller, Wolfgang Vogel, 1999 Verlag Eugen Ulmer GmbH & Co.

Ales, lagers et lambics: la bière, Mario D'Eer, 1998, Trécarré and BièreMAG, Canada.

Home Brewing, The CAMRA Guide, Graham Wheeler, 1993 CAMRA Ltd.

Good Beer Guide 2001, CAMRA Ltd.

All About Beer magazine

Dictionary of Beer & Brewing, Dan Rabin and Carl Forget, 1998 Brewers Publications

Belgium, Holland & Luxembourg, Tim Webb, 1998 CAMRA Ltd.

Brew Your Own British Real Ale At Home, Graham Wheeler and Roger Protz, 1998 CAMRA Ltd.

The medical consequences of alcohol abuse A Great & Growing Evil, 1987 The Royal College of Physicians

Bock, Darryl Richman, Brewers Publications

Northern France, Arthur Taylor, 1998 CAMRA Ltd.

Brew Classic European Beers At Home, Graham Wheeler and Roger Protz, 2001 CAMRA Ltd.

CAMRA Dictionary of Beer, Brian Glover, 1985 Longman Group Ltd.

What's Brewing, CAMRA Ltd.

CAMRA campaign publicity and external policy documents.

The Internet.

à la bière *(French; culinary)* with beer; e.g. coq à la bière: 'chicken with beer'.

AA *(abbreviation)* Alcoholics Anonymous: a voluntary organisation of people who have alcoholic dependency, who meet for self-help in counselling and group therapy. The organisation has branches in most sizeable towns and has national and international support.

∂-acid *(abbreviation)* alpha acid: the main component of the bitter flavour in the hop flower, contained in the alpha resin. Hops are often ranked by their alpha acid content. Hops with a very high alpha acid content can be coarse in bitterness.

Aass oldest Norwegian brewery, established 1834.

AAU *(abbreviation)* alpha acid unit: a measurement of the potential hop bitterness, expressed by the percentage of alpha acid in the alpha resin.

Abbaye *(French)* very strong, top-fermenting beer, naturally-conditioned in the bottle, traditionally produced by the Trappist abbeys in Belgium and across the Dutch border. Similar 'abbaye' brews in imitation of the Trappist style are made by conventional Belgian breweries.

Abbey Ales Ltd. small brewery in Bath. When launched it was the first new brewery in Bath for more than 40 years.

Abbey beers beers brewed by commercial breweries in the Trappist style.

Abbeydale a craft brewery set up in 1996 in Sheffield, UK.

Abdijbieren *(Flemish)* Abbey beers: beers brewed in the Trappist style in Belgium and The Netherlands by commercial breweries.

abgefüllt von *(German)* bottled by.

abraded barley ground barley. See adjuncts.

abrasion the process of grinding.

absolute alcohol pure, undiluted ethyl alcohol. Formula: C_2H_5OH.

Abt one of the strongest Belgian ales (12 per cent alcohol), produced in the Trappist style by the abbey of St Sixtus at Westvleteren. Besides Abt (abbot) there are also Prior and Pater.

ABV *(abbreviation)* alcohol by volume – a measure of the percentage of alcohol in a finished beer.

ABW *(abbreviation)* alcohol by weight – a measure of the alcohol content in a beer (standard in the United States of America). The European measurement ABV is approximately 25% greater.

Aca a maize beer of Peru, thought to have been first brewed over 2000 years ago.

acceleration the act of speeding up a process e.g. of the fermentation period. In order to satisfy CAMRA's definition of a pure beer there should be no deliberate acceleration of the fermentation period.

accelerometer an instrument for measuring acceleration.

acerbic *(beer evaluation)* having a harsh, bitter or astringent taste.

acetaldehyde a volatile liquid resulting from the breakdown of sugars during fermentation. Also known as ethylaldehyde. Formula: CH_3CHO.

acetaldehyde *(beer evaluation)* having a cidery or fresh green apple aroma and aftertaste: a by-product of fermentation.

acetate esters *(beer evaluation)* acetic acid esters, producing a solvent flavour.

acetic *(beer evaluation)* having a vinegary aroma and taste.

acetic acid a colourless, pungent liquid, which, in its impure, dilute form is vinegar. Acetic acid is the breakdown product of the oxidation of alcohol, most easily brought about by the action of the bacterium acetobacter, which is ever-present in the air. Any beer left exposed to air will eventually turn into a malt vinegar. Formula: CH_3COOH.

acetobacter an aerobic bacterium which turns ethyl alcohol to acetic acid.

Achouffe a Belgian spiced beer.

acid any compound which yields a corrosive solution containing hydrogen ions.

acid malt *(brewing)* a type of prepared malt (usually pale malt, to which lactic acid is added before kilning) which used to be used to lower the pH of the mash. Archaic, although possibly still used by some small micro brewers.

acid rest *(brewing)* a period of time during the mashing process in which the mash is held at between 35°C and 40°C to lower its pH. Archaic and not good brewing practice. This process relies on the fact that infection in the mash will progress rapidly, thus forming organic acids such as acetic, lactic and butyric, thereby lowering the pH. Not to be recommended.

acidic *(beer evaluation)* having a sour aftertaste, usually caused by acetic acid or lactobacillus contamination.

acidification the process of making a solution acid i.e. to make the pH value fall below 7.

acrospire embryonal barley plant within the husk.

activator a substance which increases an enzyme's rate of activity.

additive any natural or artificial chemical substance which is added to a beer to alter its taste, colour, extend its shelf life etc. See adjunct.

Adelscott a novelty beer from France.

Adelshoffen a brewery (part of the Pêcheur group), which brews 'Bière au Malt a Whisky' since it is brewed from malt kilned with peat.

ad-humulone an alpha acid.

adjunct *(brewing)* brewing ingredients, notably flaked maize, rice or wheat, or various sugars, which are added to the brew at various stages to make up a cheaper grist or to give a special flavour to the brew. The use of suitable adjuncts also reduces the nitrogen content of the beer which improves physical stability without the need for additives.

Adnams Southwold brewery committed to brewing cask ale and running unthemed pubs. The earliest recorded brewing on the Sole Bay Brewery site was in 1396 by Johanna de Corby.

Adriaan Brouwer Bierfesten a Belgian beer festival held annually in June in Oudenaarde.

adsorbent *(brewing)* any substance which adsorbs. Typically adsorbents are used pre or during filtration to adsorb nitrogenous material which could lead to in-package hazes.

adsorption substance *(brewing)* see adsorbent.

aeration *(brewing)* the process of adding oxygen (either as oxygen gas or air) to wort prior to fermentation to ensure an active initial yeast growth.

aerobic growth phase *(brewing)* the promotion of initial rapid growth of the yeast. This phase precedes the anaerobic phase (where alcohol and carbon dioxide are produced).

aftertaste *(beer evaluation)* the taste sensation after swallowing. May last between 20 seconds and many minutes.

agar-agar *(brewing)* a gelatinous substance obtained from seaweed. Its primary use is as a gel base for cultivating microbial cultures.

aged ales the collective term for beers which are set aside in large oak casks for prolonged maturation after primary fermentation.

aged flavour *(beer evaluation)* having an off-flavour, often stale – like that of cardboard or vegetable.

agglutination the clumping together of cells.

aging maturation.

agitation the act or process of stirring.

AGM *(abbreviation)* Annual General Meeting. The Campaign for Real Ale is a democratic organisation and holds an annual meeting for the election of officials and the debating of policy issues.

AHA *(abbreviation)* American Homebrewers' Association.

air (to) to ventilate the barley between steeps.

air lock *(brewing)* a one-way valve which allows excess carbon dioxide to be expelled during fermentation, whilst preventing contaminants from entering the fermenting vessel. Also known as fermentation lock.

air pressure a beer dispense system which involves the application of compressed air onto the surface of the beer in the cask, forcing the beer up to the counter through an extractor syphon. The system is little-used in England but still used in Scotland, where it operates in conjunction with tall founts.

air rest the ventilation of the barley between steeps.

air space the space between the surface of the liquid and the top of the container. Also called headspace.

airtight having been sealed so as to prevent air from entering or escaping.

Aitken a tall fount: a tall pillar-tap mounting stationed on a bar, used to dispense traditional beers in Scotland.

Al-Anon a voluntary support organisation for relatives of alcoholics. There are branches in most sizeable towns and the organisation has both national and international support.

Alcazar a micro brewery operating out of the Fox & Crown pub in Basford, Nottingham, UK and trading as Real Alcazar Ltd.

Alchemy Brewing Co. small Surrey-based brewer since 1998.

alcohol common or ethyl alcohol (ethanol). The main intoxicating component in fermented drinks. It is a waste product of the digestion of sugar by yeast. Formula: C_2H_5OH.

alcohol by volume a measure of the percentage of alcohol per volume of a finished beer. Often the alcohol by volume and the original gravity are the same. A higher alcohol by volume is an indication of a well attenuated beer. A lower alcohol by volume is an indication of residual sugars remaining in the beer. Abbreviation: ABV. ABV = (original gravity − final gravity) ÷ 75.

alcohol by weight a measure of the alcohol content in a beer (standard in the United States of America): the percentage weight of alcohol per volume of beer. The European measurement, alcohol by volume, is approximately 25% greater. Abbreviation: ABW.

alcohol content   the amount of alcohol contained in a drink. This can be specified in a variety of ways: directly in percentage by weight or volume (not the same, since alcohol is lighter than water), in several systems of 'degrees': degrees proof, degrees Plato, degrees Balling or indirectly by quoting the original gravity.

alcoholic   containing or relating to alcohol e.g. an alcoholic drink.

alcoholic *(beer evaluation)* having a warming aftertaste. In stronger beers having a wine-like flavour.

alcoholic   a person with a physical dependence on alcohol.

alcoholic strength   the measurement of the alcohol content of a beer given in percentage of alcohol by weight.

Alcoholics Anonymous   a voluntary organisation of people who have alcoholic dependency, who meet for self-help in counselling and group therapy. The organisation has branches in most sizeable towns and has national and international support. Abbreviation: AA.

alcoholism   the physical dependence on alcoholic drink. The medical evidence is conflicting as to whether this disorder is primarily physiological or psychological. See also heavy drinker; safe levels; units of alcohol.

alcoholometer *(brewing)* an instrument for measuring the percentage of alcohol by weight or volume. See hydrometer and sacharometer. Note that direct measurement of alcohol by density measurement is seldom accurate.

ale   a type of beer fermented with the top-fermenting ale yeast, Saccharomyces cerevisiae. In Anglo-Saxon times, the words 'beor' (beer) and 'ealu' (ale) were interchangeable. Divergence in meaning occurred in the late 16th century, when 'ale' came to imply an alcoholic drink made from malt without hops, and 'beer' implied the hopped beverage. This distinction is still implicit in current phrases such as 'mild ale' (not 'mild beer'), but 'ale' does not now imply that the drink is unhopped.

ale barrel   a barrel containing 32 Imperial gallons.

ale brewer   someone who brews ale. In the Middle Ages the term applied to brewers of unhopped spiced ales and not to beer brewers, who used hops for brewing.

ale bush   a traditional sign for a public house. From the 14th Century a garland of evergreen plants, usually ivy, would be hung at the top of a pole erected outside a tavern, to indicate that ale was available.

ale conner   a mediaeval official whose job it was to judge whether or not an ale was fit for consumption.

ale draper   the keeper of an alehouse.

ale drapery mediaeval name for a public house.

ale jug   a beer mug.

ale passion *(slang)* a hangover.

ale yeast   top-fermenting   yeast (Saccharomyces cerevisiae). Ale yeasts work at higher temperatures than lager yeasts and rise to the top of the fermenting vessel.

aleberry a mediaeval drink of mulled ale served with bread.

alehouse mediaeval name for a public house, referring to the room where the ale was sold and not to the adjacent brew house where the ale was brewed.

Alemaster zymopure   conventional liquid yeasts.

Ales of Kent Chatham-based brewery with a 5-barrel brew plant. Live since June 1999.

aleurone a protein in plant cells.

alewife   a brewster.

Algarroba beer a type of beer brewed in Central and South America.

alginate *(brewing)* an ester or salt of alginic acid, used as a head retention agent. To satisfy CAMRA's definition of pure beer no synthetic chemical substitutes for alginates should be used.

alginic acid   *(brewing)* a cream-coloured extract from kelp used as a head retention agent.

alkali   a soluble base or a solution of a base.

alkoholfritt øl *(Norwegian)*   alcohol free beer.

All Nations historic homebrew house in Madeley, Shropshire, which was founded in 1789.

All Saints Brewery   dates back to 1825 but has only brewed intermittently in recent years. Owned by Samuel Smith of Tadcaster.

Alley Kat Brewing Company   craft brewery in Edmonton in Canada.

all-extract beer a beer brewed using only malt extract.

all-grain beer   a beer brewed using only malted barley.

all-malt beer   a beer brewed from only malted barley without additional adjuncts or refined sugars.

Allied Breweries formed   in   1961 through the merger of Ind Coope, Ansells and Tetley Walker to create Britain's largest drinks' group. In 1978 merged with food firm Joe Lyons to form Allied Lyons.

Allsopp   one of the historic names in British brewing. Founded at Burton in 1709, it merged with Ind Coope in 1934, and traded as Ind Coope

Allsopp until 1959. Name revived for Allied's East Midlands and East Anglia company in 1985.

Almond   former brewery near Wigan taken over by Burtonwood in 1968 and used as a wine and spirit company. In 1984 Burtonwood revived the name for a few pubs and introduced a hoppier version of their own bitter, called Almond's Best Bitter.

alpha acid   the main component of the bitter flavour in the hop flower, contained in the alpha resin. Hops are often ranked by their alpha acid content. Hops with a very high alpha acid content can be coarse in bitterness. Abbreviation: ∂-acid. 'Low' = approx. 2 to 4%; 'medium' = approx. 5 to 7%; 'high' = approx. 8 to 12%.

alpha acid unit   a measurement of the potential bitterness of hops, expressed by the percentage of alpha acid in the alpha resin. Abbreviation: AAU.

alpha amylase   an enzyme which converts starch into sugar.

alpha resin   a soft resin present in the hop flower. Known also as humulone.

Alt   German beer style centred on Düsseldorf in the northwest. The word means 'old', since the dark copper-coloured beer is brewed by the traditional top-fermentation method. Alt is a rare German ale, not a lager.

Altrincham   a Brewing Company in Altrincham, launched in 2000.

Amarit   a Thai lager.

amateur brewer   a homebrewer.

amber beer   any beer which has an amber colour.

amber lager   a lager style loosely based on the Vienna lager styles, usually darker and more fully flavoured than standard pale lagers. A style favoured by lager brewers in the United States.

amber malt   mild ale malt kilned at 100-150°C (212-302°F) and allowed to cool slowly in order to attain the desired colour. It has a poor extract value. Colour: 40-60 EBC.

ambient temperature   the external surrounding temperature.

Ambrée   a Wallonian dryish pale ale (5-8% abv).

American beer   beer made using decoction mashing.

American gallon   a unit of capacity equal to six pints Imperial measure (3.79 litres).

amine   a volatile substance in beer occurring when at least one hydrogen atom of ammonia is replaced by organic groups.

amino acids organic compounds which contain at least one amino group and at least one carboxyl group. Amino acids are fundamental constituents of all proteins.

Amstel famous Dutch brewery which was taken over by its Amsterdam rival, Heineken, in 1968.

Amusements with Prizes trade jargon for slot machines: electronic gambling machines in pubs. CAMRA is concerned that these noisy electronic amusement machines have a damaging effect on the traditional character of many pubs. Abbreviation: AWP.

amylase any enzyme which hydrolyses starch into glucose, maltose and dextrins.

anaerobic fermentation *(brewing)* the fermentation phase where yeast respires without using oxygen. This phase results in the production of alcohol and carbon dioxide and very low growth rates. Also called anaerobic phase.

Anchor Steam small San Francisco brewery which produces its beers using the unique American fermentation method, by which long shallow pans called clarifiers are used. The pressure released when the casks are tapped is said to have given the lively beers the 'steam' tag.

Ancient Druids first homebrew pub (using malt extract) set up by a regional brewery, Charles Wells of Bedford, in 1984 in Cambridge.

Ancient Order of Frothblowers an informal organisation of pub-goers, active in the 1930s, mixing social activities with the collection of large sums for children's charities.

Anderson Valley Brewing Company a Californian brewery famous for its American-style amber ale.

Anheuser-Busch the world's largest brewing company, based in St Louis, Missouri, which produces the American Budweiser.

anhydrous alcohol absolute alcohol.

anker a ten-gallon cask. Very rare.

Ansells Birmingham brewery which merged with Ind Coope and Tetley in 1961 to form Allied Breweries. Twenty years later it lost its Aston brewery. All Ansells beers are now brewed at Burton.

antioxidant a reducing agent, which, when added to bottled beer, delays oxidation and so extends shelf life.

appealing *(beer evaluation)* having a pleasant look, aroma or taste.

appearance *(beer evaluation)* the overall look of a beer, including clarity, colour and head.

APPLE   *(Campaign; abbreviation)*
Apple & Pear Produce Liaison
Executive. The committee within
the Campaign for Real Ale that deals
with cider and perry. APPLE repre-
sentatives keep up with producers
of these traditional drinks, organise
their availability at festivals and
help in the preparation of CAMRA's
Good Cider Guide.

Arcen   a Dutch stout.

Archer   the symbol of Home Brewery
of Nottingham.

Archers Ales Ltd.   one of the premier
regional breweries in the south of
England, founded in Swindon in
1979.

Argyle   small   Edinburgh   brewery
established in 1982 as the Leith
Brewery.

Arkells   established real ale brewer in
Swindon. Brewing since 1843 and
still a 'family' firm.

Armstrong rake   a rotating mechanical
stirrer, which can be fitted to the
base of a mash tun to thoroughly
mix the grist.

aroma   *(beer evaluation)* the pleasing perfume given off by a beer,
produced by the raw ingredients or
fermentation.

aroma hops   finishing hops. Hop varieties with a low alpha acid content,
considered to have a mellow
flavour and aroma. Usually used as

late hops. 'Low' denotes a 2 to 4%
alpha acid content. Also known as
late hops.

AroMac   a New Zealand beer brewed
by McCashin's Breweries, using the
new 'white wine aroma' hop variety
Nelson Sauvin.

aromatic   *(beer evaluation)* having a
distinct, pleasing aroma.

Arran   Isle of Arran brewery, opened
in May 2000 by husband and wife
team.

Artisanale   *(French)* craft-brewed beer.

artist   *(slang)* an experienced drinker.

Arundel   brewery   producing   beers
from authentic Sussex recipes since
1992.

ASBC *(abbreviation)* American Society of
Brewing Chemists.

ascomycetes   a genus of fungi which
includes yeast.

Ash Vine   Somerset brewery since 1987,
now in Frome with a 25-barrel
brewhouse.

Ask if it's Cask   *(Campaign)* campaign
launched by CAMRA in March,
2001 to urge drinkers to "ask if it's
cask" next time they visit a pub, in
an attempt to get lager lovers,
smoothflow drinkers and wine con-
noisseurs to discover the taste of
real ale and thus keep the British
beer market safe for the future. The
'Ask if it's Cask' campaign is the

biggest generic promotion of British real ale since the industry campaigns in the 1950s.

aspirating valve   a device that allows the beer drawn from a cask to be replaced by CO_2 at atmospheric pressure. The aspirating valve is used to maintain the condition of beers that have to remain in cask for more than a few days. Also known as a demand valve or cask breather. A poor replacement for good cellar management. CAMRA believes that beers kept using an aspirating valve should carry a notice at the point of dispense informing the drinker of the use of such a device.

Aston Manor   Birmingham brewery set up in 1983, concentrating on supplying packaged beers to wholesalers and supermarkets. It bought the Highgate Brewery in June 2000.

astringent   *(beer evaluation)* having a tannic, vinegar or tart aftertaste. An astringent mouthfeel results from phenols, oversparging, long mashes, and hops which have been boiled too long.

attemperate (to)   *(brewing)* to control temperature.

attemperation   *(brewing)* a method of controlling the temperature at which the fermentation of beer takes place. This temperature is very important – too low and the fermentation may stop ('stick'); too high and it may 'race', producing unpleasant flavours.

attemperation coils   *(brewing)*   a heat exchanger. Many fermenting vessels are fitted with attemperation coils through which suitably cold water can be circulated to control the temperature of the fermenting wort.

attemperator   *(archaic; brewing)* an ice-filled device used prior to the introduction of attemperation coils to maintain a constant fermentation temperature.

attenuation   *(brewing)* the reduction in specific gravity during wort fermentation i.e. the extent to which the fermentable sugars have been used up by the yeast. No beer ever has the sugars used up entirely. Highly attenuated beers have a very dry palate; less attenuation yields a sweet beer.

attenuation limit   *(brewing)* theoretical limit of fermentation.

au fût   *(French)* on draught.

aucun additif chimique *(French)* with chemical additives.

Augustiner   the oldest brewery in Munich, Southern Germany, noted for its adjoining beer garden. It was originally part of a monastery, and there is still a monastic brewery called Augustiner over the Austrian border in Salzburg.

austere   *(beer evaluation)* having a harsh or an astringent taste.

autolysis the digestion of dead yeast cells by enzymes produced by the yeast cells themselves.

automatic revolving sprays   *(brewing)* sparge arms: rotating, perforated tubes which spray hot liquor on to the top of the grains to flush out the last fermentables.

autovac   an old style of beer engine, formerly used in parts of the north. The beer overflowing the glass into the drip tray is re-cycled through the pump. Also known as an economiser.

auxiliary an association of publicans' wives primarily devoted to charitable and social activities.

auxiliary finings *(brewing)* a fining agent added to aid protein coagulation during the final stages of boiling. See Irish moss.

Aviemore brewery which started brewing in July 1997. The company also owns Tomintoul.

avoine   *(French)* oats.

awn the bristles on barley, oats, wheat etc. Also called beard.

awn cutter   a machine used to cut the awns from malted barley.

AWP *(abbreviation)* slot machines, known in the trade as amusements with prizes.

Axe Vale small brewery set up in Colyton, Devon, in 1983.

Aying   a German Pilsener.

Ayinger   a German dark beer; also a German wheat beer.

B & T Shefford-based Banks & Taylor brewery, founded in 1981 and restructured in 1994. Brews a wide range of beers.

°B *(abbreviation)* Balling. A measure on the Balling saccharometer.

b-acid *(abbreviation)* beta acid: a bitter hop resin, almost insoluble at normal wort pH values.

back *(semi-archaic; brewing)* any holding vessel. Term reserved now for hop back, yeast back and racking back.

bacteria typically unicellular microorganisms which can infect wort and beer.

Badger Hall & Woodhouse Ltd. : a well established brewer, founded in 1777 as the Ansty Brewery; now brewing from its site at Blandford St Mary under the Badger trade name. Bought King & Barnes of Horsham in 2000.

bail the wire securing the ceramic top of a swing-top bottle.

Baileys small brewery set up in 1983 near Malvern in Worcestershire.

balance tank *(brewing)* a tank used to balance the flow of beer to a filling machine. When the filling stops the balance tank fills to avoid shock waves being sent back to the main tank (which avoids sediment disturbance).

Ballard's country brewery on the Sussex/Hampshire border, set up in 1980.

Balling a measure on the Balling saccharometer. Abbreviation: °B.

Balling a saccharometer first engineered in the mid 19th Century. It is calibrated for 17.5°C (63.5°F) and graduated grammes per hundred, giving a direct reading of the percentage of extract by weight per 100 grammes solution. See Plato.

Bamberg the Bavarian home of 'smoked' beer.

Bamberg beer a Rauchbier.

banana ester *(beer evaluation)* isoamyl acetate. Having an aroma of bananas or nail polish remover.

Banfield Ales a small brewery in Burrough-on-the-Hill, Leicestershire, started in May 2000 using a 4. 5-barrel plant.

Banks & Taylor see B & T.

Banks's the trading name of The Wolverhampton & Dudley Breweries.

bar a counter between customers and staff, where alcoholic drinks are served.

bar a public room within a pub, as in public bar.

bar often personalised name for a hostelry, especially in Scotland and Ireland, as in Bennet's Bar.

bar (to) to ban from a pub. Bad news 'you're barred!'. Licensees have an absolute right to bar anyone they choose. CAMRA supports the right of licensees to refuse to serve individuals in order to maintain orderly premises.

bar towel a rectangle of towelling material used to decorate bar counters and usually featuring the name of a brewery in its design.

Barge & Barrel brewery in Elland set up by White Rose Inn. See pub groups.

barkeeper an alternative name for a barman.

barley a cultivated cereal, which edible grain, when partially germinated and then kilned produces the malt for brewing. Unmalted barley is also used to add colour.

barley syrup *(homebrewing)* a cheap, substitute for malt in inferior (though not necessarily cheaper) beer kits.

barley wine a strong, rich and sweetish ale, usually over 1060 OG, dark in colour, with high condition and a high hop rate. Extended fermentation times render most barley wines potent in alcohol. As a result and because of their heavy palate, they are usually sold in 'nip' bottles containing one-third of a pint.

barm *(brewing)* the frothy yeast head which rises to the top of a fermenting vessel. Only seen these days in traditional open vessels. Most commercial breweries use conical fermenters and a yeast which sediments to the cone.

barm (to) *(archaic; brewing)* to pitch yeast.

barmaid a woman who serves in a pub.

barman a man who serves in a pub.

barmy beer young beer, still fermenting. 'Barmy' hence came to be used to describe someone lightheaded or slightly mad.

Barngates Cumbrian brewery set up in 1997 for the in-house use of The Drunken Duck Inn. In 1999 a brand new 5-barrel plant was installed and the brewery became a separate limited company.

Barnsley brewery, formerly the South Yorkshire Brewing Company. It brews with an old yeast culture from the town's long-defunct Oakwell Brewery.

baron a Belgian beer glass holding 50 centilitres.

barrel a 36-gallon cask. Not a general name for any other size; the general term is cask.

barrelage the usual way of describing a pub's (or brewery's) business in barrels (36 gallons) per week or per year.

barrelage agreement   a common method for a brewery to tie up a so-called 'free' outlet in return for a 'cheap' loan. The pub or club agrees to buy a certain annual barrelage.

barrelling the act of transferring the beer to barrels.

Barren   brewery in Devon, set up in 1984 in Silverton.

barrique   *(French)* a hogshead.

Bartrams eponymous Suffolk brewery of Marc Bartram since April 1999.

Barum   house brewery of the Reform Inn in Barnstaple, Devon.

Bass national brewer in the UK, encompassing many traditional breweries incorporated over hundreds of years. Brands include Carling, Tennent's Lager and Caffrey's. Carling was the first beer ever to break the three million barrel per year barrier. In 2000 Bass was taken over by Interbrew but the UK government ruled that the takeover should be 'unravelled' because it was against the interests of the consumer – the position espoused by CAMRA.

Bass Museum   museum of beer and brewing in Burton on Trent. The on-site microbrewery brews and bottles the famous Worthington's White Shield bottle-conditioned beer. Claims to be the 'national' museum of beer and European funding has helped create an impressive visitor attraction.

batch fermentation   *(brewing)* the brewing of beer in batches. There have been attempts at designing continuous production methods, but none have proved successful.

batch sparging   *(brewing)* the use of a "batch" of sparge water to flush out wort from the mash as distinct from a semi continuous spray of water on the top of the mash as the wort is drawn off.

Bateman   Lincolnshire family brewery in Wainfleet, serving 'Good Honest Ales' since 1874, originally only to local Fenland pubs, but now nationwide. Trading name: George Bateman & Son Ltd.

Bates   small brewery set up in Bovey in 1983.

Bath Ales Bristol brewery begun in 1995 and upgraded to a full steam, 15-barrel plant in 1999.

Batham   small Black Country family brewery which brews its distinctive beers behind one of the most remarkable brewery taps in Britain, the Vine or 'Bull and Bladder' in Brierley Hill, which declares across its front 'Blessing of your heart, you brew good ale'. Trading name: Daniel Batham & Son Ltd.

Battersea Watney pub brewery, Prince of Wales, Battersea.

Baudelot cooler　a type of wort cooler in home-brewing, comprising horizontal cold water copper pipes.

Bavaria　a Bundesland in Southern Germany, which produces almost a third of the world's hop crop.

BB　initials usually given to light West Country bitters from breweries like Palmers and St Austell. Popularly known as 'Boys Bitter'. Occasionally means 'Best Bitter', as in the BB produced by Harveys of Lewes, Sussex.

bead　the bubbles in a beer which rise to the surface.

Beamish　an irish stout.

Beamish & Crawford　Eire brewer dating back to 1792 in Cork City. Known for Beamish stout.

beard　awn.

Beards　Sussex brewery taken over by Greene King.

Beartown Brewery Ltd.　Brewery in Congleton, Cheshire, set up in 1994.

Beauty of Hops　a competition sponsored annually by the National Hop Association of England and HRI to encourage British brewers to use hops more imaginatively and promote increased consumer awareness of the importance of hops to beer appreciation.

Beck　famous German brewer, based in Bremen, and the largest exporter of German beer. Widely known for its Beck's Bier, which is brewed in strict accordance with the Reinheitsgebot.

Beckett's Brewery Ltd.　Basingstoke brewery, set up in March 1997.

Beecham's Bar & Brewery　training establishment within St Helens College of Further Education, St Helens, Merseyside.

beer　the generic term for a non-distilled alcoholic drink produced by fermentation of a wort derived from mashed malted barley grain. The word beer derives from the Old English word baerlic for barley. See ale.

beer and skittles　pleasure or enjoyment.

beer belly　a bulging stomach caused by drinking too much beer.

beer blast　*(American slang)* a party at which vast amounts of beer are drunk.

beer brewer　a person who brews beer.

beer can　a sealed thin metal container with a ring pull for beer.

Beer Drinkers' Manifesto　*(Campaign)* a series of demands laid down by CAMRA to be raised with brewers, pub groups, MPs, MEPs, members of the Scottish Parliament and the Welsh Assembly aimed at saving British breweries, halting the loss of rural pubs, encouraging the development of organic beers and stopping mergers and takeovers which threaten consumer choice.

Beer Engine (The) a Devon brew pub set up in 1983.

beer engine suction handpump, usually mounted on the counter, used to draw beer from the cellar. It is designed to pull up a half-pint at each stroke.

beer festival a day or number of days during which the organised events revolve around the consumption of beer and promotion of beer styles.

beer garden an outdoor drinking area originally having an abundance of floral decoration, now often characterised by swings, sandpits and other games. See Biergarten.

beer kit *(homebrewing)* a 'starter pack' for the homebrewer usually comprising a tin of hopped, liquid malt extract and a packet of dried yeast. The best quality kits are 100% malt extract. Inferior kits have high proportions of other ingredients. See barley syrup.

beer life the shelf life of beer. See antioxidant.

beer mat a mat, originally made of cork and now usually of thin card, for soaking up beer spillage under glasses. Beer mats are regarded by breweries as promotional material and by many customers as collec-table items; the word 'tegestologist' has been coined for a collector of beer mats. Also known as coaster.

beer nog a drink made with stout heated with dark rum, eggs and honey.

beer on tap draught beer.

beer orders government regulations covering licensing laws and consumer choice in pubs. The law helps maintain choice in pubs tied to big brewers.

beer parlour licensed premises in Canada where beer can be sold and drunk.

beer pull the handle of a beer engine.

beer pump beer engine.

beer spoilage bacteria *(brewing)* bacteria such as acetobacter or lactobacillus which can utilise alcohol and/or sugar to produce organic acids such as acetic acid or other undesirable organic chemicals.

beer Stein a German drinking vessel, similar to a stone tankard, traditionally covered with a hinged metal lid.

beer tasting wheel *(beer evaluation)* a flavour wheel, developed to standardise beer tasting terminology, to enable brewers and beer lovers world-wide to communicate the flavours they experience.

beer taxation the duty the Chancellor of the Exchequer levies on beer. One of drinkers' main concerns at budget time every year. See bootleg lager.

beer volatiles *(brewing)* esters, aldehydes, higher alcohols and other organic chemicals. All affect flavour (for better or worse). They are the by-products of fermentation and can be controlled by correct fermentation procedures and adjuncts.

Beerex an exhibition of beer i.e. a beer festival.

beer-up *(slang)* an alcohol-inspired get-together.

beery smelling or tasting of beer.

Beisl *(Bavarian; Austrian)* 'no frills' pub.

Belgian aromatic an aromatic malt which yields a strong malt aroma.

Belgian pale ale pale ale using roasted, slightly caramelised malts and Saaz or Northern Brewer hops.

Belhaven Brewing Co Ltd. Scotland's oldest independent brewery, situated at Dunbar on the east coast, near Edinburgh.

Belle Vue a mass-marketed Belgian Gueuze beer from Brussels.

belly the widest diameter (centre) of a cask. Also known as bilge.

Belvoir Brewery Ltd. Leicestershire brewery set up in March 1995.

Beowulf Brewing Co. Birmingham's only independent brewery.

Bergkirchweih *(German)* an annual beer festival held during Whitsun in Franconia.

Berkeley Brewing Co. small brewery in Gloucestershire, set up in 1994 in an old farm cider cellar.

Berliner Weisse the bottle-conditioned white beer of Berlin. Brewed using wheat to a low alcohol content of about 3 per cent, this refreshing summer drink is often laced with woodruff or raspberry syrup ('mit Schuss') to give a violent green or red colour. The slightly sour taste comes from the addition of lactic acid bacteria during fermentation. It is traditionally drunk with a straw from a large sundae dish type glass. The major brands are Kindl and Schultheiss.

Berliner Weisse mit Strippe Berliner Weisse served with a chaser of Kümmel (caraway) spirits.

Berrow small Somerset brewery at Burnham-on-Sea which started brewing in 1982.

best ubiquitous description for many milds and bitters, often where no 'ordinary' is offered. One of the best-known Bests was Courage's Best Bitter.

beta acid *(brewing)* bitter hop resin, almost insoluble at normal wort pH values. Also called beta resin; lupulone. Abbreviation: b-acid.

beta amylase *(brewing)* an enzyme, found in germinated barley, which hydrolyses starch into sugars.

beta glucan *(brewing)* a sticky substance found in abundance in unmalted grains of barley. It is an important component in beer foam, but in excess can cause filtration problems both in wort and beer.

beta resin a bitter hop resin, almost insoluable at normal wort pH values. Also called beta acid.

bevel the upper surface at the top of a barrel or cask.

beverage general term for any drink but often understood, in context, to refer to beer.

bevvy *(slang)* term, especially in the north, for beer or drink. Derives from beverage.

Biddy Early Brewery CAMRA member Dr Peadar Garvey, an industrial chemist, launched this brewery Inagh, Co. Clare, Eire, to provide drinkers with an alternative to the mass produced beers.

Bier *(German; Dutch; Flemish)* beer.

bier van spontane gisting *(Flemish)* beer, fermented spontaneously.

Bierbauch *(German)* beer belly.

bierbrouwerij *(Dutch)* brewery.

bière *(French)* beer.

bière blanche *(French)* white beer.

bière blonde *(French: 'light beer')* pale-coloured beer.

bière bock *(French)* a category of beer in France which includes all beers with an original gravity of between 3.3 and 3.9° Régie.

bière brune *(French: "brown beer")* dark-coloured beer.

bière d'Abbaye *(French)* abbey beer.

bière d'epeautre *(French)* beer which has undergone a secondary fermentation.

bière de choix *(French: "choice beer")* a category of beer in France which includes all beers with an original gravity of between 4.4 and 4.6° Régie.

bière de garde *(French: "keeping beer")* the smooth 'laying-down beer' of Northern France, which appears in wine-shaped, wire-corked bottles. The best example is Jenlain and the best-known St Leonard.

bière de luxe *(French: "luxury beer")* a category of beer in France which includes all beers with an original gravity of 4.4° Régie and higher.

bière de malt *(French: "malt beer")* a lightly fermented, low-alcoholic drink from malt extract.

bière de Mars *(French: "March beer")* special Spring beers, traditionally only available in March.

bière de moine *(French)* abbey beer.

bière de Noël *(French: "Christmas beer")* rich, festive beer.

bière de nourrice *(French: "nourishing beer")* a bière de malt: a lightly fermented, low-alcoholic drink from malt extract.

bière de table *(French: "table beer")* sweet, low alcohol pale or dark ale. A category of beer in France which includes all beers with an original gravity of between 2 and 2.2° Régie.

bière forte *(French)* strong beer.

bière spéciale *(French:"special beer")* a category of beer in France which includes all beers with an original gravity of between 5 and 7° Régie.

bière sur lie *(French)* bottle-conditioned beer, with yeast sediment.

bière trappiste *(French)* Trappist beer.

Biergarten *(German: "beer garden")* an outdoor drinking area. The south German city of Munich is famous for its numerous Biergärten, some of which seat several thousand people.

Bierglas *(German)* beer glass.

Bierkeller *(German)* beer cellar: a bar in a cellar.

Bierkrug *(German)* a glass, pottery, pewter etc. tankard or beer mug.

Bierkrügel *(Austrian)* a beer jug or glass holding half a litre.

Bierseidel *(German)* Bierkrug.

Bierstube *(German)* a small pub (Kneipe).

Biersuppe *(German: "beer soup")* soup made from water, beer, flour, sugar and eggs.

Big Lamp Newcastle-upon-Tyne brewery started in 1982 and relocated in 1996 to a 55-barrel former water pumping station.

Bigfoot Traditional Ales Ltd. brewery housed in former farm buildings in Lincolnshire.

BII *(abbreviation)* British Institute of Innkeeping: an organisation of pub licencees and managers. The institute provides training courses and lobbies on behalf of its members.

bilge the widest diameter (centre) of a cask. Also known as pitch.

bine the climbing stem of the hop plant.

Bird in Hand Cornish pub housing the Wheal Ale Brewery Ltd.

Biobier *(German)* bottled beer which is unfiltered, unpasteurised or has undergone a secondary fermentation in the bottle.

bionda *(Italian: 'blonde')* a light, lager-style beer.

Birell low-alcohol lager from Hurlimann. Unlike other near beers, Birell uses a special yeast so that only 0.8 per cent alcohol is produced.

birra *(Italian)* beer.

birreria   *(Italian)* pub.

biscuity   *(beer evaluation)* having a malty flavour. A description often applied to pale ales.

Bishop   small brewery in Somerset set up in 1984, brewing Bishop's PA (1037) and Best Bitter (1041).

Bitberger a German Pilsener.

bitter *(beer evaluation)* having an after-taste associated with hops, malt and yeast.

bitter highly hopped ales, ranging from 1030 to around 1055 OG. Within this range, the term is most commonly applied to 'drinking bitters' in the 1032-1044 OG band. The most common type of draught ale, low in carbonation.

Bitter a cask-conditioned organic beer brewed by Pitfield (London).

bitter ale popular name for low-gravity bitters, particularly in the south-west and South Wales.

Bitter End Brew Pub Cumbrian brew-pub founded in 1995.

bitter resin soft resin.

bitter wort *(brewing)* the wort after it has been boiled with bittering hops for an hour or more.

bittering capacity *(brewing)* a measure of the alpha acid content of hops.

bittering hops *(brewing)* hops which are put into the brew kettle at the beginning of the boil for bittering and preservation purposes. Also known as copper hops; kettle hops; high alpha hops.

bitterness units   *(brewing)* standard method of measuring the amount of bitterness in a given volume of beer. Abbreviation: BU.

black *(beer evaluation)* a colour definition. A beer that is described as 'black' is often a deep red when viewed with a strong light.

black and tan stout mixed half and half with bitter or mild. Also called a mix.

black beer a syrupy bottled malt extract chiefly produced by Mathers of Leeds, with 7 per cent alcohol. Usually mixed with lemonade to make 'Sheffield Stout' or with rum to make the original, lethal 'rum and black'.

Black Bull Brewery   Haltwhistle brewery.

Black Dog Brewery Whitby brewery which plays on Bram Stoker's writings in its beer names.

Black Eagle a cask-conditioned organic beer, brewed by Pitfield (London).

Black Isle Scottish brewery launched in December 1998.

black malt a specially malted barley achieved by roasting kiln-dried malt. Used mainly for adding colour and a dry roast barley flavour to mild beers, porters and stouts. Colour 1250-1500 EBC.

Black Russian a beer cocktail made with stout and vodka.

Black Sheep Brewery Masham-based brewery set up in 1992 by Paul Theakston, a member of Masham's famous brewing family.

Black Velvet a beer cocktail made with equal amounts of stout and champagne. The poor man's alternative is stout and cider.

Blacksmith a beer cocktail made with stout and barley wine.

bladdered *(slang)* a description of someone who is drunk.

Blanchfields of Fakenham Norfolk brewery, brewing since November 1997 using a custom-made 2.5 barrel plant.

blandit *(Campaign)* word coined by CAMRA to describe smoothflow beers that look like real ale but are dead beers when they leave the brewery. "Beware of the blandits!"

blanket pressure *(brewing)* a low pressure of carbon dioxide applied to beer in the cask to prevent its exposure to air. Not supported by CAMRA because of the difficulty in controlling the amount of gas taken up by the beer, which makes it 'fizzy'.

blathered *(slang)* description of someone who is drunk.

Blencowe Brewing Company Rutland brew pub.

Blewitts Devon brewery, expanded from brewpub origins.

Blitz-Weinhard brewers of one of the strongest United States beer, Olde English 800 (7.5 per cent alcohol), from Portland, Oregon.

BLO *(Campaign; abbreviation)* Brewery Liaison Officer: a CAMRA official who acts as a point of contact with a brewery's management.

Blonde Wallonian medium strong pale ale (6-8% abv).

blonde in the black skirt (or dress) *(Irish)* Guinness.

blossom alternative term for the hop cone: the hop flower head, rich in aromatic resins, oils, tannins and acids.

blotto *(slang)* description of someone who has drunk themselves into a state of unconsciousness.

blow-by *(homebrewing)* see blow-off.

blow-off *(homebrewing)* a method which removes residues and carbon dioxide during fermentation through a plastic tube, one end of which is fitted into the mouth of a carboy and the other in a bucket of sterile water. Also known as blow-by.

BLRA *(abbreviation)* Brewers' and Licensed Retailers' Association: the trade association of British brewers and pub operating companies, dating back to 1822. It represents the beer and pubs industry to Government, both in the UK and in Europe. Formerly Brewers' Society.

Blue Anchor thatched brew pub in the centre of Helston, Cornwall; once a monks' resting place in the 15th century. Its ales are known locally as Spingo.

Blue Cow inn and brewery opened March 1997.

Blue Star the sign of Newcastle Breweries' beers.

Boag's Tasmanian brewery. J Boag & Son has run a brewery on the Esk River in Launceston Tasmania since 1881. Tours and tastings available.

Boat Brewery West Yorkshire brew pub.

Bobby Ales beers from Randall of Guernsey.

Bock the name of a strong German lager style, originating in Einbeck, Lower Saxony, but now more associated with Munich. Dark and pale types are produced with an alcohol content of at least 6 per cent. The beer is often linked with seasonal festivals, particularly in autumn or May (Maibock). Bock also means billy goat, and a goat's head often features on the label. In a typical act of European unity, Bock (or Bok) in France and Belgium means a beer of low strength. See also Doppelbock and Eisbock.

Boddingtons Manchester brewery, next to Strangeways prison. 'Boddys' famously fought off Allied Breweries' takeover attempt in 1970 and then swallowed Oldham Brewery. Purchased by Whitbread and turned into a national beer 'brand'. Typical of a real ale in name that isn't real when purchased at the supermarket.

Bodicote Brewery brewery founded in 1982 at the Plough Inn, Bodicote, Banbury.

body *(beer evaluation)* a mouthfeel characteristic referring to the sensation of fullness in the mouth, usually indicative of the malt content and degree of fermentation, and rated from light to heavy or full. The higher the malt content, the fuller the body. The greater the attenuation the lighter the body.

boil *(brewing)* the stage in the brewing process where the wort is heated with the hops in the copper.

boiler *(brewing)* a large, electric vessel in which the wort is boiled.

boiler feed water *(brewing)* water, which has been chemically treated to avoid scaling in boilers.

boiling fermentation *(brewing)* a fermentation which seems to boil due to the eruption of large gas bubbles. Attributed to various causes. Seldom seen.

bokbier *(Dutch)* a dark, relatively strong bitter Dutch beer style, based on the German Bockbier.

Bokbier Festival an annual Dutch festival of bokbiers organised by PINT and held in Amsterdam at the start of November.

Bokkøl *(Norwegian)* Norwegian bock beer (max. 7.0% ABV).

bootleg (to) to sell illicit alcohol. See bootleg lager.

bootleg lager cheap, fizzy lager which has been smuggled into the country to be sold illicitly, to avoid paying excise duty. CAMRA believes that over a million pints a day are smuggled into Britain and therefore urges a cut on excise duty, which would reduce the bootleggers' profit and make it a less desirable commodity.

bootlegger someone who profits by the smuggling in and selling of illicit alcohol.

booze *(slang)* any alcoholic drink.

boozer *(slang)* a pub.

boozer *(slang)* a noted drinker.

boozer's hooter *(slang)* a large red nose (from having had too much to drink).

booze-up *(slang)* an alcohol-inspired get-together.

Border brewery opened in 1992 in Berwick upon Tweed on an historic brewing site.

Borve Brew House brewhouse since 1983, once on the Isle of Lewis, now in Huntly, Aberdeenshire.

Boston Experience Ltd. brewery in Woking, Surrey, brewing beers to American recipes.

botanical beer non-alcoholic brews produced in the days of the Temperance Movement, especially popular in areas where that movement was strong, such as Birmingham. Old stone jars from 'botanical' breweries are sometimes found among pub bric-a-brac.

bottle cap a crimped metal bottle top.

bottle-aged bottle-conditioned. Some bottle-conditioned ales benefit from ageing in the bottle.

bottle-conditioned a bottled beer in which a secondary fermentation takes place in the bottle as a result of yeast left in the mixture after boiling. Such beers have a sediment and must be stored and served with care. CAMRA encourages all producers of bottle-conditioned beers to state "Real Ale in a Bottle" clearly on their labels.

bottle-fermentation *(brewing)* a deliberate secondary fermentation in the bottle to produce a natural condition. It also forms a sediment and beers should be poured carefully.

bottom fermentation *(brewing)* fermentation in which the yeast cells sink to the bottom of the vessel. This is a property of certain yeast strains, in particular those such as Saccharomyces uvarum (formerly Saccharomyces carlsbergensis), used for lager production. Bottom fermentation is conducted at low temperature, 10°C (50°F) or below, thus being considerably slower than top fermentation. These yeasts form less of a head than Saccharomyces cerevisiae, the top-fermenting ale yeasts.

bottoms the sediment left at the bottom of the cask, which contains yeast and finings and any hops that have been added to the cask. Also known as lees.

bouchon *(French)* a cork.

bouquet *(beer evaluation)* the characteristic fermentation aroma of a beer.

bracteole the petals of the hop flower.

Bragdy Ty Bach the smallest brewery in the world (allegedly), based in North Wales.

Bragdy Ynys Mon Anglesey brewery established in 1999.

Bragwr Arbennig O Ceredigion Welsh brewery with a range of bottle-conditioned beers.

Brains independent Cardiff brewery trading under the name of SA Brain & Company Ltd.

Brakspear brewery based on historic site in Henley upon Thames. The 19th Century brewhouse and tun room still incorporate the two-tier dropping system of fermentation.

Bramling Cross a British aroma hop with a 6.5-7.5% alpha acid content.

bran *(beer evaluation)* having a biscuity flavour, usually resulting from the use of pale and crystal malts.

Brand a Dutch Pilsner; a Dutch lager and a Dutch double bock.

brand name a trade name identifying a manufacturer or a product. CAMRA condemns the use of brand names made famous by cask-conditioned ales to promote keg, including nitro-keg, beers.

Brandy Cask pub and brewery, set up in Pershore, Worcestershire in 1995.

Branscombe Vale brewery set up in 1992 in two cowsheds owned by the National Trust.

brassée *(French)* brewed.

brasserie *(French)* brewery.

brasserie a bar serving food and drink.

Brau AG   the brewing giant of Austria, based in Linz, which also owns the Schwechat brewery near Vienna where Anton Dreher produced the first bottom-fermenting lager beer in 1841.

Brauerei   *(German)* brewery.

Brauhaus   *(German)* brewery.

Bräu   *(Bavarian; Austrian)* referring to any specific type of beer.

Bräu   *(Bavarian; Austrian)* pub.

Bräustüberl   *(Bavarian; Austrian)* a small inn.

bready   *(beer evaluation)* having a cooked or pasteurised flavour.

break   *(brewing)* visible particles of protein and other matter which form in the wort during boiling and cooling.

break   *(brewing)* flocculation.

breathalyser   a device to enable police to gauge the alcohol consumption of a motor-vehicle driver.

brettanomyces lambicus   a yeast strain used in Belgium for lambic beers.

brew   *(brewing)* generically the batch of beer from inception to packaging.

brew   the wort.

brew (to)   *(brewing)* to make beer and ale from malt and other ingredients by steeping, boiling and fermenting although in a commercial brewery additional stages are involved: milling, mashing, lautering and casking (bottling or canning).

brew pub   a pub which brews beer on the premises.

brewer   a person or concern that brews beer for home consumption or commercially.

breweriana   collectable bits and pieces from breweries or pubs. Breweriana includes beer mats and other point-of-sale advertising devices, beer bottle labels, ashtrays etc. Items are worth more if the products or companies they advertise are now defunct. Auctions of breweriana have been known to raise considerable sums.

Brewers' Association of America   trade association of brewery owners in America, dedicated to the best interests of the brewing industry.

Brewer's Gold   a German general purpose hop variety with a 5-6% alpha acid content.

brewer's paddle   *(homebrewing)*   a long-handled instrument used for stirring the beer. Unlikely to be used in commercial brewing.

brewer's yeast   *(brewing)* yeast, in dry or liquid form, which has been prepared for brewing.

Brewers' & Licensed Retailers' Association   the trade association of British brewers and pub operating companies, dating back to 1822. It represents the beer and pubs industry to Government, both in the UK and in Europe. Formerly Brewers' Society. Abbreviation: BLRA.

brewers' droop *(slang)* a flaccid penis (from having drunk too much alcohol).

Brewers' Gold a UK bittering hop with an alpha acid content of 8-9%.

Brewers' Guild a charitable brewer's organisation. Now amalgamated with the Institute of Brewing.

Brewers' Society   see Brewers' & Licensed Retailers' Association.

brewers' Tudor an architectural style favoured for suburban pubs in the early 20th century, with gables and exposed timbers, imitative of manor houses. Often clumsily carried out, and derisorily referred to as Tudorbethan.

brewery a place where beer or ale is brewed.

brewery-conditioned *(brewing)* beer which has undergone fermentation in the brewery and then been conditioned and filtered and usually pasteurised; i.e. tank or keg beer. Brewery conditioning is a process against which CAMRA actively campaigns.

Brewery Liaison Officer *(Campaign)* a CAMRA official who acts as a point of contact with a brewery's management. Abbreviation: BLO.

Brewery on Sea Ltd. Sussex brewer established in 1993. Beers called Spinnaker.

brewery tap traditional term for a pub built into town breweries. The nearest pub to a brewery is also often referred to as the 'brewery tap'.

Brewex Britain's brewing trade fair held every few years. Best known for its beer championships, in which most British breweries compete for medals.

brewhouse *(brewing)* the area of a brewery where the beer is mashed and brewed.

Brewhouse Brewery established in 1980 on Poole High Street, Dorset.

brewing *(brewing)* the process of making wort, boiling it with hops and fermenting it into beer.

brewing liquor *(brewing)* water, natural or treated with calcium and magnesium sulphate, for mashing and brewing. Also called brewing water; mashing liquor; liquor.

brewing water *(brewing)* water.

Brewlab based at the University of Sunderland. It provides training and analysis for the brewing industry and conducts research into problems of small scale production and beer character Brewlab provides technical support to CAMRA.

Brewing Research International membership organisation supporting the work of commercial brewers. Abbreviation: BRI.

brewing yeast *(brewing)* a prepared yeast for brewing, which can be obtained in both dried and liquid forms.

brew-length *(brewing)* the number of barrels in a plant.

brewster Mediaeval term for a brewer, referring particularly to a female brewer.

Brewster Sessions the annual licensing court which deals especially with license renewals and amendments to permitted hours. Sessions begin in early February each year. Licences are usually granted en bloc. Government's intention is to move licensing authority away from the courts – see licence reform.

Brewster's Brewing Co Ltd. brewery set up in 1998 by brewster Sara Barton. Based near Melton Mowbray, Leicestershire.

Bridge of Allan brewery formed in 1997 in the Scottish Forth Valley. Visitor centre.

Bridgewater Ales Ltd. Manchester based brewery, originally established in Salford in 1999.

bright *(beer evaluation)* having good clarity.

bright beer a chilled, filtered and often pasteurised beer. See finings.

Briscoe's brewery established in owner's house in 1998 in Otley, West Yorkshire, for one barrel brews.

British Columbian a general purpose hop with a 7% alpha acid content.

British Guild of Beer Writers a subscription based organisation of journalists, authors and photographers.

British Institute of Innkeeping an organisation of pub licencees and managers. The Institute provides training courses and lobbies on behalf of members. Abbreviation: BII.

British Standard Pipe thread 3/4" is the modern standard for beer lines. Abbreviation: BSP.

Broadstone Brewing Company Ltd. started brewing in September 1999 in Retford.

Broughton Ales Ltd. Scottish borders brewery founded in 1979 and later taken over by Whim Brewery owner. Produces mainly bottled beers.

brouwerij *(Dutch; Flemish)* brewery.

brown ale bottled sweetish mild ale; usually dark, low in alcohol, and very lightly hopped. There are exceptions (e.g. Newcastle Brown Ale and Sam Smith's Strong Brown Ale) which are of higher gravity and flavour, but are still sweet rather than bitter.

Brown Betty a chilled beer cocktail made with ale and Cognac and flavoured with cloves.

Brown Cow Brewery home-based Selby brewery supplying local pubs.

brown malt smoked malt, traditionally kilned over a hardwood fire. The most commonly used malt in Britain prior to the Industrial Revolution. Now a rarity. Colour 150 EBC.

browning reactions *(brewing)* see Maillard reactions.

Bruce creator in the 1980s of the chain of homebrew pubs in London, under the 'Firkin' banner.

bruinnen Belgian brown ale.

Brune strong Wallonian brown ale (7-9% abv).

Brunswick Brewing Co. Derby tower brewery attached to the Brunswick Inn, the first railwaymen's hostelry in the world.

Brussel's lace a term to describe the head that clings to the side of the glass.

bryggeri *(Danish; Norwegian)* brewery.

Bryncelyn Brewery a brewery since 1999 in the Swansea (Wales) area.

BSP *(abbreviation)* British Standard Pipe thread: 3/4" BSP is the modern standard for beer lines.

BU *(abbreviation; brewing)* bittering units: standard method of measuring the amount of bitterness in a given volume of beer.

BU:GU ratio *(abbreviation; brewing)* the ratio of bittering units to gravity units in a specific beer.

Buckley formerly Wales's oldest brewery, in the rugby stronghold of Llanelli. The site was closed in 1997 after its acquisition by SA Brain & Company Ltd.

Bud or Budweiser. American lager brewed under licence around the world.

Budvar a Czech beer. The original and best Budweiser, claim the Czechs. The well-known American beer takes its name from Budvar's home town of Ceske Budejovice (Budweis in German), which supplied the Bohemian court with beer in the 16th century. American 'Bud' is lagered for a minimum of three weeks; Budvar say their original is conditioned for over three months. The Czech beer is also stronger.

Budweiser an international best-selling lager, from Anheuser-Busch of St Louis, launched in 1876 as the first American national brand. It takes its name from the Czech town of Ceske Budejovice (Budweis in

German), and is brewed with rice as well as malted barley, and fined over beechwood chips.

Buffy's Brewery Norfolk brewery established in 1993.

bulk barrel a barrel holding 36 gallons.

Bullion a general purpose hop with a 5.3 alpha acid content.

Bullmastiff Brewery award-winning craft brewery run by two brothers in Cardiff (Wales) area.

Bunce former brewery. See Stonehenge.

bung *(brewing)* the hole in the head of a cask. Also called bunghole.

bunghole *(brewing)* aperture in the head of a cask through which a cask is filled with beer before being closed by the shive.

burnt *(beer evaluation)* having a 'roasted' flavour. A characteristic of dark and roasted malts (used to brew stouts) or over-caramelised wort, produced through excessive boiling.

burnt sugar caramel: brown roasted sugar used to add colour and sweetness to dark beers.

burr a union or cupped nut which secures the two parts of a pipe joint in place.

Burton Ale once a general name for beers brewed at Burton-upon-Trent, England's capital of brewing, where the well water, with its high concentration of calcium and magnesium salts, makes it ideal for brewing strong pale ales. From 1976, the name was chiefly used for Ind Coope's premium cask bitter (1047.5).

Burton Bridge small brewery set up in 1982 in England's brewing capital, Burton-upon-Trent, supplying local pubs and its own brewery tap.

Burton Union a traditional open fermentation method, during which the beer rises out of large oak casks through swan-neck pipes into long troughs for use in pitching into following brews. It is this system which made Draught Bass famous, but they closed their Union rooms in the early 1980s. The future of Burton Union open fermenters is uncertain following a Health & Safety Executive ruling which states that open fermenters must be covered to exclude all carbon dioxide from the fermenting room. See Marston, Thompson & Evershed PLC.

burtonise (to) *(brewing)* the adding of chemicals by brewers to their brewing liquor (water) to make its composition identical to that in Burton. One of the main factors which made Burton-upon-Trent such an important brewing centre was the quality of the local well water. This contains a range of salts, most especially gypsum (calcium sulphate), which are perfect for producing pale ales and bitter beers.

Burtonwood Brewery Warrington brewery founded by the Eldridge family as the Green Dragon Brewery in 1837, but now operating as part of the Thomas Hardy group.

bush brass or, more commonly, plastic insert in wooden casks for the keystone or shive.

Bush Beer one of the strongest Belgian beers (12% abv); a Wallonian speciality beer, similar to barley wine. Also called Scaldis.

Bush house traditionally an ale house which was set up at a country fête or fair to produce beer for that event.

Butcombe Brewery Ltd. a successful Bristol-based brewery since 1978.

butt a cask with a capacity of 108 gallons, no longer used for beer. The wine trade, however, still uses the name for large casks of a variety of sizes.

butterfly valve *(brewing)* an automated modern disc valve having the same diameter as the pipe, used in commercial brewing.

butterscotch *(beer evaluation)* a buttery or toffee aftertaste, resulting from the fermentation product diacetyl.

buttery *(beer evaluation)* a butter-like aftertaste, caused by bacteria or by a reduced fermentation time.

Butts Brewery Ltd. Hungerford-based brewery set up in converted farm buildings in 1994.

butyl acetate an ester which produces the fruit odours in beer.

byg *(Danish)* barley.

°C *(abbreviation)* centigrade or Celsius: denoting a measurement on the Celsius scale.

Cains popular name for the Robert Cain Brewery Ltd. , Liverpool's best known brewery, established on its current site in 1850.

Calandria *(brewing)* a device placed internally in the copper to vigorously boil the hopped wort during brewing.

calcium bicarbonate a substance which contributes to temporary water hardness, but which can be removed in part by boiling the water. Also called calcium hydrogen carbonate. Formula: $Ca(HCO_3)_2$.

calcium sulphate a substance which contributes to permanent water hardness. See burtonise. Formula: $CaSO_4$.

Caledonian Brewing Company Edinburgh's main brewery, established in 1869. Still brews in direct-fired open coppers.

cambier mediaeval term for a brewer in northern France.

Cambrinus Craft Brewery small enthusiast brewery in Knowsley.

Camerons Brewery Company established in Hartlepool in 1865; recently a very successful brewer of real ale.

Campaign for Better Beer consumer group in the United States, launched by the American Homebrewers' Association, whose aim is to promote quality beer. See CAMRA.

Campaign for Real Ale *(Campaign)* CAMRA. A successful consumer campaign launched in 1971 as a reaction against keg beers, foisted on the public by the national brewers, who dominated Britain and threatened to crush the remaining independent companies. CAMRA's current members are involved not only in fighting for real choice in every bar, but also in opposing brewery takeovers, pub closures, restrictive licensing hours, soaring beer prices, etc. CAMRA is the only voice of the drinker in an industry still dominated by national combines. CAMRA celebrated 30 years of campaigning in 2001, the same year that it launched the 'Ask if it's Cask' invitation to drinkers to try the superior taste of real ale.

Campaign for the Revitalisation of Ale *(Campaign)* the former name of the consumer campaign CAMRA. Formed on March 16th 1971 by four young drinkers Graham Lees, Mike Hardman, Bill Mellor and Jim Makin.

CAMRA *(Campaign; abbreviation)* The Campaign for Real Ale, a successful consumer campaign launched in 1971 as a reaction against keg beers, foisted on the public by the national brewers, who dominated Britain and threatened to crush the remaining independent companies. CAMRA's current members are involved not only in fighting for real choice in every bar, but also in opposing brewery takeovers, pub closures, restrictive licensing hours, soaring beer prices, etc. CAMRA is the only voice of the drinker in an industry still dominated by national combines.

CAMRA Investment Club *(Campaign)* a scheme which operates like a unit trust, investing members' monthly payments in a range of breweries and pub chains. Open to CAMRA members.

Cannon Royall Brewery cider house in Worcestershire, which turned to real ale brewing in 1993.

Canstatter Wasen a German beer festival held in the autumn in Cannstatt, Stuttgart.

cant short D-shaped planks in the head of a wooden cask.

Cantillon an unusual Belgian museum brewery, producing wild lambic beers, in Anderlecht, Brussels, which invites visitors in the summer.

Cantillon a lambic beer.

cap bottle or crown cap.

capper any instrument used to seal bottles with crown stoppers.

capping machine automated mechanical device for sealing bottles with crown stoppers.

Captain Cook Brewery Middlesbrough brewery, which began brewing in 1999.

caramalt pale crystal malt: lightly kilned malt used for lager brewing. Also called Carapils.

caramel brown roasted sugar used to add colour and sweetness to dark beers.

caramel *(beer evaluation)* having a toffee-like flavour, produced by scorched sugar or dark crystal malts – freshly malted barley grains, which are stewed at moderate temperatures before drying.

caramel malt pale crystal malt: lightly kilned malt used for lager brewing. Also called carapils.

caramelisation *(brewing)* the sugar-browning process.

caramunich malt a dark crystal malt, which imparts a sweet roasted flavour.

carapils *(brewing)* lightly kilned malt used for lager brewing. Also called caramalt.

caravienna malt *(brewing)* a crystal malt, which imparts a light roasted flavour.

carbohydrate any of a large group of organic compounds which comprise carbon, hydrogen and oxygen atoms. Sugars and starches from the malt are the main carbohydrates in beer. The more the beer is attenuated, the lower the residual carbohydrate level. Such 'dry' beers can be suitable for some diabetics, although the high calorie content makes them useless for weight control.

carbon dioxide an inert gas. It is one of the waste products produced by the yeast as it consumes the sugars in the wort (another is alcohol). Much of the carbon dioxide is given off from the fermenting vessels (big breweries often sell it as a by-product), but much remains dissolved in the beer. This is essential to give the beer its condition. The amount of carbon dioxide that enters the beer depends upon the beer temperature and the carbon dioxide pressure; cooling the beer or increasing the pressure will increase the amount dissolved. There are strict controls governing carbon dioxide emissions in breweries and regular checks by Health & Safety Executive inspectors. Traditional open top fermentation systems could be banned. Formula: CO_2.

carbonade *(culinary)* beef and onions stewed in beer.

carbonated *(beer evaluation)* gassy, due to the presence of dissolved carbon dioxide.

carbonation the addition of carbon dioxide to beer to produce a fizzy drink, either by injecting the finished beer with carbon dioxide, priming, krausening or pressure fermentation. See also gush.

carboy a large, narrow-necked glass, earthenware or plastic bottle, sometimes with a protective wicker, plastic or wooden casing.

Carling O' Keefe the Canadian brewery whose former owner, Eddie Taylor, helped create the Bass Charrington giant in Britain through a series of brewery takeovers in the 1960s to gain outlets for his Black Label lager. See Bass.

Carlow Brewing Company small brewery in Carlow, Eire. The beers are based on original Celtic recipes.

Carlsberg Denmark's first lager beer, launched on November 10th 1847 by Captain J. C. Jacobsen in Valby, a small town on a hill overlooking Copenhagen. It was named after his son Carl and 'berg', which when translated means 'hill'.

Carlsberg A'S formerly United Breweries Ltd. and formed in 1970 by the merger of Denmark's two most important breweries, Carlsberg and Tuborg.

Carlsberg Brewery in the UK, the Northampton brewery set up in 1974 to brew all the Carlsberg needed for the UK market.

Carlsberg-Tetley a wholly-owned subsidiary of Carlsberg of Copenhagen, the famous Danish brewers who perfected the bottom-fermenting yeast, Saccharomyces carlsbergensis, now used by lager brewers everywhere.

Carlton United the giant of the Australian brewing industry, best known in its Melbourne home for its Carlton and Victoria beers, but outside Australia famed for its 'tubes' of Fosters.

Carnaval de Binche an annual beer festival held on the Sunday, Monday and Tuesday before Ash Wednesday in Binche, Belgium.

Carnegie a tall fount: a tall pillar-tap mounting stationed on a bar, used to dispense traditional beers in Scotland.

carrageen a variant spelling of carragheen.

carragheen *(brewing)* a seaweed sometimes used to clear the beer during brewing. Also referred to as Irish moss.

caryophylline a component of hop oil.

Cascade an American aroma hop containing approximately equal amounts of alpha and beta acids. The resulting aroma is spicy, floral and citrus (especially grapefruit).

cask the general name for any of the barrel-shaped containers of various sizes used for traditional draught beer. Casks were traditionally made from wooden staves with an iron hoop, but nowadays stainless steel and aluminum casks are also used. See piggin, pin, firkin, kilderkin, barrel, butt and hogshead. See Robinson's. CAMRA believes that all casks should be clearly labelled with the racking date of the beer.

cask breather a device that allows the beer drawn from a cask to be replaced by CO_2 at atmospheric pressure. The cask breather is used to maintain the condition of beers that have to remain in cask for more than a few days. Also known as a demand valve or aspirating valve. A poor replacement for good cellar management. CAMRA believes that beers kept using a cask breather should carry a notice at the point of dispense informing the drinker of the use of such a device.

cask condition the quintessence of real ale – the beer put into the cask must contain enough yeast for a slow secondary fermentation to take place. This fermentation produces the subtle matured flavours that distinguish real ale from dead 'keg' beers.

casking the racking of beer.

Cask Marque a plaque displayed outside a pub awarded to the publican to indicate that he or she has passed a series of intensive tests in keeping and dispensing real ales.

Cask Marque Trust a non-profit-making organisation which operates an independent accreditation scheme to recognise excellence in the service of real ale.

cask washer *(brewing)* a machine for cleaning casks in the brewery.

cask wood the pieces of timber used for making casks. The wood is usually oak.

cast (to) *(brewing)* to empty a vessel.

Castle Eden Brewery Hartlepool-based independent brewery once more after a management buy-out from Whitbread in 1998.

Castle Rock Brewery Nottingham's only full-mash brewery, created by a partnership between Tynemill and Bramcote Brewing Company at today's site close to Nottingham's historic castle rock.

Castlemaine-Tooheys two of Australia's best-known brewers, Castlemaine of Brisbane and Tooheys of Sydney, which merged in 1980 to challenge the might of Carlton United.

cast-out wort *(brewing)* the wort which has been run off after boiling.

catalyst a substance which increases the rate of a chemical reaction. Enzymes are catalysts.

caudel a warming drink made from sweetened ale, flavoured with saffron and heated. Can also be made with spiced wine.

cauliflower head *(brewing)* the thick layer of dirty yeast which billows up during top fermentation and must be skimmed.

Caythorpe Brewery purpose-built brewery, opened in 1997 in the Nottingham area.

cellar a room in a pub, traditionally below ground to maintain a steady low temperature, where the beer casks are stored. The modern cellar is now often at street level and air-conditioned. 13°C (about 55.5°F) is the ideal cellar temperature.

cellarage an area of the cellar.

cellarage the storing of the casks to allow conditioning and maturation.

cellarman the person responsible for receiving, stacking and generally looking after the storage of the beer casks.

cellulase an enzyme in barley which initiates fermentation.

Celsius denoting a measurement on the Celsius scale. Abbreviation: °C.

Celsius scale the centigrade scale: a scale of temperature in which 0°Celsius represents the freezing point of water and 100°Celsius represents the boiling point of water.

Centennial an American general purpose/bittering hop variety with a high alpha acid content. Spicy, floral, citrus aroma.

centigrade denoting a measurement on the centigrade scale. Abbreviation: °C.

centigrade scale the Celsius scale. A scale of temperature in which 0° represents the freezing point of water and 100° represents the boiling point of water.

centilitre one hundredth of a litre. Abbreviation: cl.

centres the longest planks in the head of a wooden cask.

centrifuge *(brewing)* a separation vessel in which the beer is made to spin rapidly: heavy sediments collect at the outside and are discharged and the cleared beer runs off from the centre to a tank.

cepovane pivo *(Czech)* draught beer.

cereal adjuncts *(brewing)* brewing ingredients, notably flaked maize, rice or wheat, which are added to the brew at various stages to make up a cheaper grist or to give a special flavour to the brew. The use of appropriate adjuncts can reduce the nitrogen content of the beer, which improves physical stability without the need for additives.

cereal cooker *(brewing)* a mash cooking vessel.

cereals *(brewing)* wheat, maize or barley.

cerne pivo *(Czech)* dark beer.

cerveza *(Spanish)* beer.

cervoise *(French)* a mediaeval French word for a beer made without hops.

cervoise de miel *(French)* beer which has been sweetened with honey.

chalk calcium carbonate, a mineral found in or added to water to make it hard and alkaline. Formula: $CaCO_3$.

Chalk Hill Brewery Norwich brewery since 1993.

Challenger a British general purpose hop with a 6.5 to 7.7% alpha acid content.

chambrée *(French)* room temperature.

Champion Beer of Britain *(Campaign)* accolade awarded by CAMRA after judging at the Great British Beer Festival, held annually in August.

Champion Winter Beer of Britain *(Campaign)* accolade awarded by CAMRA after judging at the Winter Beer Festival held annually.

Chariot a type of malt.

Charles Wells Ltd. a brewing company which brews in Bedford at the Eagle Brewery, the largest independent family-owned brewery in the UK, established in 1876 and still run by descendants of the founder.

chaser usually a beer drunk straight after a spirit.

cheesy   *(beer evaluation)* having a smell or taste of cheese. This characteristic is undesirable in beer and results from old and oxidised hops.

Cheriton Brewhouse   purpose-built Hampshire brewery.

cherry beer   Kriek: a Belgian Gueuze beer in which the second fermentation has been caused by adding black cherries or cherry juice.

chevalier   *(French)* a beer glass with a 2.5 litre capacity.

Chevallier barley   alternative name for two-rowed barley.

chewy   *(beer evaluation)* a cloying sensation, produced by a strong body or high protein levels.

Children's certificate   an official document granted by licensing authorities to pubs deemed to have facilities suitable for children. CAMRA supports a version of the children's certificate system and believes that there should be no requirement in law that children should have to take a meal to use the premises, or to leave by a given time before the pub closes. CAMRA believes that the emphasis should be on the publican's decision whether to admit children.

chill (to)   *(brewing)* to cool beer, almost to freezing, which causes the suspended proteins to separate. They can then be filtered to leave a clear product. 'Chilled and filtered' is a common description for brewery-conditioned bright beer.

chill haze   the cloudy appearance of cask-conditioned beer which is allowed to get too cold. This cloudiness is caused by protein separation and will not settle out. Whilst spoiling the appearance of the beer, it makes no appreciable difference to the flavour.

chillproof beer   any beer which has been chemically treated to prevent chill haze.

chillproofing   *(brewing)* the act of treating any beer to enable it to withstand low temperatures without chill haze forming.

Chiltern Brewery   Buckinghamshire brewery since 1980. Shop and museum on site.

Chimay   the classic Belgian Trappist ales produced by the Abbaye of Chimay on the French border. The three famous bottle-conditioned beers – Capsule Rouge (6.6 per cent alcohol), Blanche (7.5), and Bleu (8.5) are distinguished by the colour of their bottle tops. The blue is even vintage-dated, reaching its peak after two years.

chimb   the projecting rim at each end of a cask.

Chinook   an American bittering hop variety. Spicy aroma.

chit   steeped barley.

chlorophenolic *(beer evaluation)* having a TCP, medicinal or plastic-like aftertaste and aroma resulting from chlorophenols.

chlorophenols chemical compounds with a pungent, medicinal taste caused by the chemical combination of chlorine and phenolic compounds during fermentation.

chocks wooden blocks used to prevent the rolling or sliding of casks while on stillage.

chocolate malt specially malted barley treated in the same fashion as black malt, but at a lower kilning temperature, used to give flavour and colour to milds, stouts and porters, and to dark European beers like Bock and Malzbier. Colour: 900-1400 EBC.

chocolatey *(beer evaluation)* having a chocolate flavour. This chocolate characteristic results from the use of dark chocolate malts, used mainly in the brewing of dark beers and stouts.

Christmas ales rich festive ales, often available in polypins, and brewed by a number of British brewers.

Church End Brewery Warwickshire brewery since 1994. Known for using unusual fruit adjuncts (banana etc.).

cidery *(beer evaluation)* having a tart fresh apple aftertaste or smell, often because of too much acetaldehyde and volatile acids.

City of Cambridge Brewery Ltd. 5-barrel brew plant which has been supplying local outlets since 1997.

clarifier *(brewing)* a substance used to remove or prevent chill haze.

clarifier a long, shallow fermentation pan used in some American breweries.

clarity *(beer evaluation)* the level of translucence of a beer.

Clark Wakefield beer wholesalers who resumed cask ale brewing in 1982. Trading name: HB Clark Co. (Successors) Ltd.

Clausthaler a low-alcohol (0.6 per cent) bottled lager imported from Germany.

Clayson Report the government report on the Scottish licensing law made in 1976, headed by Dr Christopher Clayson. It led to the passing of the 1976 Licensing (Scotland) Act, which allows pubs to apply for regular extensions to permitted hours and so remain open all day in Scotland. See Scottish Hours.

clean (to) to remove dirt and leftover deposits. Bacteria and spores cannot be removed by cleaning.

Clearwater Brewery T o r r i n g t o n brewery based in former St Giles in the Wood Brewery since January 1999.

clear wort *(brewing)* wort which is not cloudy with sediment.

Clockwork Beer Co. trading name for Glasgow micro-brewery.

closing time the moment when the publican is required to have you leave his premises. This is usually straight after drinking-up time, averaging ten minutes after official last orders have been served.

cloudy *(beer evaluation)* hazy, due to suspended microorganisms or protein precipitates.

cloyingly sweet *(beer evaluation)* having a sugary aftertaste, caused by the sugars not having been fully fermented or excessive primings.

Club of the Year *(Campaign)* a competition held annually to recognise and reward British clubs which can prove a "Commitment to Real Ale". Abbreviation: COTY.

club room a facility – a private room where folk clubs, pigeon societies, angling clubs, and even CAMRA branches can meet and drink while pursuing their hobby or business without disturbing regular customers. Now in decline.

Cluster an American and Australian general purpose/bittering hop with an alpha acid content of 7.0-7.5%.

Coach House Brewing Company Warrington brewery founded in 1991.

coaching inn an old hostelry once used as a regular picking up and setting down point for horse-drawn coach passengers, usually offering accommodation, food, and stabling for replacement horses. Often characterised by arched entry passages leading to a rear yard.

coaster a beer mat.

Cobra an Indian lager.

cohumulone an alpha acid.

coigns Scottish term for chocks; wooden blocks used to prevent the rolling or sliding of casks while on stillage.

cold break *(brewing)* the flocculation of protein and polyphenol molecules during wort cooling.

cold sedimentation *(brewing)* the clearing of beer by exposure to chilling. Potential haze particles coagulate and precipitate.

Coles Family Brewery brewery near Carmarthen since 1999.

collar the space between the tops or measure line of a glass and the beer surface.

colour of beer an attribute of beer, defined using the EBC scale or the SRM.

Concertina Brewery South Yorkshire brewery in the cellar of a club in Mexborough. Brewing since 1992.

condition the amount of carbon dioxide present in beer. To be palatable, beer must contain dissolved carbon dioxide; this gives it freshness and sharpens the flavour. Too much condition leads to frothiness and over-sharp flavours (as with keg beers); too little condition makes the beer flat and insipid. Maintaining the correct condition is a skilled job. See natural condition.

conditioning *(brewing)* the maturation of beer after it has been removed from the fermenting vessel.

conditioning tanks *(brewing)* commercial steel vats for conditioning the beer.

cone the moving part of a cask tap, operated by the handle.

conical (fermenter) *(brewing)* a modern type of fermenting vessel in the shape of a tall cylinder with a tapered lower end.

Coniston Brewing Co. 10-barrel brewery, which won the Champion Beer of Britain competition in 1998 for its Bluebird Bitter.

consultant brewer a brewer who does not brew, but gives advice/consultancy on brewing.

container beer another term for keg or bright beer: pressurised brewery-conditioned or processed beer, usually pasteurised.

continuous fermentation *(brewing)* a continuous production method by which wort was passed continuously through a concentration of yeast, instead of being fermented in batches. This design, and others, have so far proved unsuccessful. In commercial brewing beer is brewed in batches.

conversion *(brewing)* the process during the mash in which natural malt enzymes change grain starch into sugar.

cooked vegetables *(beer evaluation)* having a corn aroma or a smell of cooked vegetables. Generally caused by slow cooling of the wort and resulting from dimethyl sulphide (DMS).

cool ship *(archaic)* a former method of cooling beer, by which the beer would be pumped into a large, shallow tank to be cooled by the surrounding air.

cooper a maker or repairer of casks, normally only applied in the context of traditional wooden casks.

Coopers Australian brewery, based in Adelaide, producing remarkable bottle-conditioned ales fermented in wooden casks.

Coors the largest single brewing plant in the world, situated in Golden, Colorado, which gained a rather folksy image for its lager because of its isolated position in the Rocky Mountains.

copper *(beer evaluation)* a colour definition.

copper *(brewing)* the brewery vessel in which the wort and the hops are boiled, producing the hopped wort that will then go into the fermenting vessels. A modern copper is a closed stainless steel tank, heated by internal steam coils or external calandria, although, as the name suggests, these vessels were formerly made of copper. A few breweries still use open coppers with direct firing. Also known as kettle.

copper finings *(brewing)* a clearing agent added to aid protein coagulation during the final stages of boiling. See also Irish moss.

copper hops *(brewing)* bittering hops put into the brew kettle at the beginning of the boil for bittering and preservation purposes.

copper oxychloride a fungicide approved and permitted by the Soil Association for hop growers.

copper sugar any brewing sugar added to the brew kettle during the boil.

copper syrup *(brewing)* a concentrated malt extract used in the copper to extend brew length or to adjust gravity.

coq à la bière *(French; culinary)* chicken in a beer sauce.

Corvedale Brewery a Shropshire brewpub.

Cotleigh Brewery Somerset brewery that started trading in 1979, in the historic brewing town of Wiveliscombe.

Cottage Brewing Co Ltd. Somerset brewery founded in 1993. Its Norman's Conquest beer took the Champion Beer of Britain title at the 1995 Great British Beer Festival.

Cottage Spring Brewery craft brewery in Cwmbran.

Country Life Brewery Devon brewery, with viewing screens so that visitors can watch the brewing process.

country pub a rural inn. Country pubs in the UK are currently closing at the rate of six a week. CAMRA believes that country pubs are essential community amenities and should be eligible to receive 50% mandatory relief on their business rates. The government passed a bill in 2001 providing a 50% reduction on business rates to sole pubs in settlements with fewer than 3,000 in habitants and with a rateable value below £9,000.

Cox & Holbrook Suffolk-based 5-barrel plant since early 1997. Emphasis on dark ales, stouts and porters.

Cox's Yard Stratford-on-Avon brewery, part of a development by large Bedford regional Charles Wells Ltd. . Regular talks.

cracking *(brewing)* the act of gently splitting the grain before mashing, to release the starch contained within the husks.

Cranborne Brewery Dorset brewery since Easter 1996.

Cream Ale an odd American brew in which a small amount of top-fermented beer is blended with lager. The main producers are Genesee of Rochester, New York.

cream flow nitrokeg: keg beer which is dispensed with a mix of carbon dioxide and nitrogen. CAMRA affirms that nitrokeg is just another form of brewery conditioned/keg beer and condemns the excessive hype surrounding such beers, which are not real ales.

cream stout a former popular name for smoother 'milk stouts', still retained by Felinfoel of South Wales for their bottled export stout (1040).

creme à la bière *(French; culinary)* a sweet beer sauce made with cream.

Crewkerne Brewery a Somerset brewery since 1997.

Cropton Brewery North Yorkshire brewpub, specialising in bottle-conditioned, additive-free beers.

Crouch Vale Essex brewery set up in 1981 near Chelmsford.

crown cap a crimped metal bottle top.

crown cork metal bottle top with a layer of cork on the inside which replaced the stopper in beer bottles; now rare itself. See crown cap.

Crown Inn Shropshire pub-brewery established in 1994.

Crusade tax the first excise duty on beer levied in England by King Henry II. All brewery equipment and sales of beer were subject to a ten per cent tax.

crystal malt high nitrogen barley malt used primarily for ale brewing, which is removed from a standard kiln and placed into another preheated kiln at a higher temperature. This process produces a glossy finish to the grain, which, when used in brewing, enhances body in beer. Also called caramel malt. Colour: 100-300 EBC.

Cuckmere Haven Brewery East Sussex brewery, which has used Harveys yeast since 1994.

cuisine à la bière *(French; Flemish)* a style of cooking using beer as an essential ingredient.

curing   *(malting)* the final stage in the malting process: barley is placed into kilns at high temperatures in order to halt germination. Also known as kilning.

cuvée   *(Flemish)* term implying a Belgian beer matured in the cask.

DAB *(abbreviation)* the largest German brewery, Dortmunder Actien. Also owns Hansa in Dortmund. Best known for its dry Export and Meister Pils. Not to be confused with DUB, Dortmunder Union.

Daleside Brewery Ltd. Harrogate brewery since 1985. Changed its name from Big End Brewery in 1992.

damson aphid a major hop pest.

dangerous levels alcohol consumption which exceeds the safe limits: generally defined as above 49 units a week for men and 35 units a week for women. See safe drinking; units of alcohol.

Danish Light a low-alcohol lager (less than 0. 6 per cent) brewed in Copenhagen.

dark a popular name for mild in South Wales.

dark bok a dark, strong, bitter Dutch beer style. See bok.

Dark Horse Brewery Ltd.
Hertfordshire brewery started in 1994 in the cellar of the White Horse pub.

Dark Star Brewing Co. set up in 1994 in the cellar of the Evening Star in Brighton.

dark straw *(beer evaluation)* a colour definition.

darkish *(beer evaluation)* a colour definition.

DarkTribe Brewery Scunthorpe brewery built in 1996 and run as a part-time business.

Darwin Brewery Ltd. Durham based brewery since 1994. Acquired Hodges Brewery of Crook, County Durham.

DE *(abbreviation; brewing)* dextrinisation equivalent: the enzymic process by which amylases hydrolyse starch into sugars. A 100% DE would be equivalent to the production of 100% glucose (dextrose).

De Dolle a Belgian dark ale.

de fermentation spontanée *(French)* spontaneous fermentation.

De Koninck a top-fermented Belgian beer, similar to German Alt, from Antwerp's only brewery. The all-malt copper ale (5.2 per cent alcohol) is unpasteurised on draught.

decoction *(brewing)* one of the two main methods of mashing (the other being infusion). Decoction is the usual system used in Europe for lager-type beers. Decoction mashing is a process of several steps (usually three) with staged temperature rises, as portions of the extract are drawn off (decocted), brought to the boil, and then returned to the mash tun. The advantage claimed for this complicated system is that different enzymes are more efficient at the different temperatures so that a more complete extraction can be obtained from the lighter malts needed for lager beers.

Deeping Ales brewery formed in 1996 on the edge of Peterborough, and subsequently bought by Kent businessman.

degrees Balling denoting a measure on the Balling saccharometer. Abbreviation: °B.

degrees Celsius denoting a unit of temperature as measured on the Celsius scale. Abbreviation: °C.

degrees Centigrade denoting a unit of temperature as measured on the Celsius scale. Abbreviation: °C.

degrees Fahrenheit denoting a unit of temperature as measured on the Fahrenheit scale. Abbreviation: °F.

degrees Lovibund denoting a unit on the scale, used by American brewers to measure the wort and colour of beer. See SRM. Abbreviation: °L.

degrees Plato denoting a unit of measurement on the Plato saccharometer, expressing the specific gravity as a percentage of extract by weight per 100 grammes solution. Abbreviation: °P.

degrees proof denoting a unit of measurement on the scale to measure the strength of an alcoholic beverage when the proof spirit measures 100°. Abbreviation: °proof.

degrees Régie a measurement on the scale used in France to measure the density of wort. 1° Régie = 2.6° Balling. Abbreviation: °R.

demand valve a device that allows the beer drawn from a cask to be replaced by CO_2 at atmospheric pressure. The demand valve is used to maintain the condition of beers that have to remain in cask for more than a few days. Also known as cask breather and aspirating valve. A poor replacement for good cellar management. CAMRA believes that beers kept using a demand valve should carry a notice at the point of dispense informing the drinker of the use of such a device.

Dent Brewery brewery set up in 1990 in a converted barn in the Yorkshire Dales.

Derwent Brewery set up in 1997 in Cockermouth, now in Silloth.

Derwent Rose Brewery micro-brewery based in Consett's oldest surviving pub (153 years old in 2001). First brewed in 1997.

desitka *(Czech)* a beer of 10° strength.

Devenish former 'seaside' brewers in the Southwest of England.

Devon Ales Ltd Alloa brewery since 1994.

dextrinisation equivalent *(brewing)* the enzymic process by which amylases hydrolyse starch into sugars. A

100% dextrinisation would be equivalent to the production of 100% glucose (dextrose). Abbreviation: DE.

dextrins   non-fermentable and slowly-fermentable sugars which contribute to the mouthfeel of beer.

dextrose   a glucose. Formula: $C_6H_{12}O_6$.

diacetyl *(beer evaluation)* a compound which gives beer a butterscotch-like aftertaste; produced by fermentation.

diastase   alpha amylase and beta amylase: enzymes which convert starch into sugar.

diastatic malt extract (syrup) *(brewing)* a malt extract, used in mashing, which contains diastatic enzymes which convert brewing adjuncts into fermentable sugars. Abbreviation: DMS.

Diätpils   *(German)* Diet Pils.

Diet Pils   beers, which suggest that they will help you slim, but don't. Although they contain less carbohydrate than non-diet beers as they are fermented for longer, to turn the sugars to alcohol, they are strong (around 6 per cent alcohol) and alcohol is considerably more fattening than carbohydrate. They are, however, ideal for diabetics.

dimethyl sulphide   an aromatic compound which imparts a corn aroma or a smell of cooked vegetables to beer. Slow cooling or contamination of the wort are the most common causes of dimethyl sulphide. Abbreviation: DMS.

Dinkel   a beer type in which dinkel malt is used instead of barley malt.

Dinner Ale a low-gravity, usually bottled beer once made by a second mash of the malt. Recommended for consumption with meals. Now rare.

dipstick   a thin rod, usually of square section, dipped into a cask through the spile hole to measure the contents. Normally scales for four different cask sizes are engraved on the four sides.

disinfect (to) to use chemicals to destroy harmful microorganisms.

dispense   a trade term for delivering the beer to the customer's glass. The means of dispense plays an important part in the final taste and quality of the beer. See also electric pump; sparkler; tall fount.

dive *(slang)* an unsavoury bar or pub. The term originally referred to public houses located below street level.

dixie a large, metal pot, which can be used in homebrewing for boiling the wort.

Dixie well-known American brewery and beer from New Orleans, with lots of jazzy marketing.

DMS *(abbreviation)* diastatic malt syrup: a malt extract, used in mashing, which contains diastatic enzymes which convert brewing adjuncts into fermentable sugars.

DMS *(abbreviation)* dimethyl sulphide: an aromatic compound which imparts a corn aroma or a smell of cooked vegetables to beer. Slow cooling or contamination of the wort are the most common causes of DMS.

dog's nose an eighteenth century mix of beer with gin or rum.

Dominion New Zealand's second-largest brewing group, based in Auckland, which first used continuous fermentation.

donkey box tiny snug capable of seating fewer than a dozen people.

Donnington Brewery brewery set up on the site of a 13th Century water-mill in 1865 in a fold of the Cotswolds near idyllic Stow on the Wold.

Doppelbock *(German: "double bock")* an extra-strong German beer style, brewed using dark malt, with an alcohol content of at least 7.5 per cent. The original double bock, produced by the Munich brewery of Paulaner, is called Salvator, and ever since the names of all Doppelbocks have ended in-ator e.g. Optimator from Spaten and Maximator from Augustiner. See also Eisbock.

doppio malto *(Italian: "double malt")* a Bock-style beer.

DORA *(abbreviation)* Defence of the Realm Act, 1915. Wartime legislation, intended only as a temporary measure, that introduced restrictions on pub opening hours for the first time, aimed at helping the war effort. The laws were consolidated in the 1921 Licensing Act, which forms the basis of current restrictions on pub hours.

dormalt a system of malting using a continuous conveyor.

Dortmunder a German beer style. Dortmund is one of the biggest brewing cities not only in Germany but also in Europe, with a beer style to match. Dortmunder Export is drier and stronger than lagers from Munich and Pilsen, with over 5 per cent alcohol.

Dos Equis *(Spanish: "two crosses")* a Vienna-style amber brew, brewed in Mexico.

downy mildew a hop disease caused by parasitic fungi.

draught a general term for any drink that is dispensed from a bulk container into smaller measures for sale, i.e. as served over the bar from a tap in a pub. Thus Draught Beer can be either cask conditioned or brewery conditioned. CAMRA opposes the promotion of canned beers as "draught" products and believes that the term should only be applied to bulk beers.

draught lambic old or young lambic, sometimes a mix of both, occasionally sold in Belgian cafés.

dray vehicle used to deliver beer. Originally horse-drawn.

Dreher, Anton Dreher's brewer. At the turn of the century Dreher's brewing empire was the largest in the world, with plants in Hungary, Czechoslovakia, Italy, and Austria, where he brewed the first bottom-fermented lager beer in 1841.

dried yeast packaged yeast used in home-brewing.

Driftwood Spars Hotel St. Agnes brewpub since 2000, although this Cornish pub and hotel date from the 17th Century.

drinking-up time the time allowed for consumption of the last drink of the session (afternoon or evening). Time allowed is 10 minutes in England and Wales, 15 in Scotland, 30 in Northern Ireland, and 15 in the Isle of Man.

drip mat a beer mat.

drip tray a metal or plastic tray fitted under beer taps to catch the overflow or slops.

dropping *(brewing)* a brewery practice by which liquid is transferred from one vessel to another by gravity.

dropping system *(brewing)* a method of brewing, which involves dropping (piping) the wort into a second fermenting vessel before fermentation has been completed (usually when the wort is half fermented). This practice provides yeast agitation to resuspend potentially flocculating yeast. Rarely used today in commercial breweries.

drum malting *(malting)* a malting system first developed in Britain in the 1950s, employing modification within enclosed tubular revolving drums.

dry *(beer evaluation)* not sweet. A dry beer is predominately bitter.

dry hopping the addition of a small quantity of fresh hops to a cask as it is filled with beer. Dry hopping adds a further aroma and bitterness to the beer, subtly different from that provided by the hops boiled in the copper. The hops floating on the beer surface also give protection from airborne spoilage organisms.

DUB *(abbreviation)* Dortmunder Union, the chief rival to DAB in Dortmund, best known for its Export and Siegel Pils. With Schultheiss of Berlin, it forms one of Germany's major brewing groups.

Dubbel a strong dark beer in Belgium and The Netherlands of approximately 6 or 7 per cent alcohol, though not necessarily in the abbey style.

Dubbelbock *(Flemish "double bock")* strong Belgian lagers in the German Doppelbock style.

Duffield Brewing Co. brewery in the cellar of the Thorold Arms in Harmston, Lincs, since 1996.

dunkel *(German: "dark")* pertaining to dark, malty, bottom-fermented beers, usually Münchener.

dunkles Weißbier *(German: "dark white beer")* a wheat beer brewed using a dark wheat malt.

Dunn Plowman small Herefordshire brewery, at its present site in Kington since 1994.

Durham Brewery brewery supplying local outlets since 1994.

Dutch pale ale a filtered or pasteurised, low to medium strength (5-5.5% abv) lager-style brew.

duty the tax levied by the Customs and Excise department on all of the beer that a brewer produces. CAMRA supports a complete revision of the excise duty payable on alcoholic drinks and seeks a two-thirds reduction in the current excise duty on beer. High levels of excise duty cause encomic and social problems as pubs and breweries are undermined by cheap imported beer. CAMRA believes the duty should be reduced to a level that removes the incentive to smuggle.

Smuggled beer threatens attempts to tackle alcoholism and underage drinking.

Duvel *(Flemish: "devil")* the golden Belgian ale from the Moortgat brewery near Antwerp, described by one beer expert as 'one of the world's greatest beers'. Duvel is a soft, bottle-conditioned ale – with a sudden punch from its 8.5 per cent alcohol.

dvanactka *(Czech)* a beer of 12 degree strength.

dwarf hops varieties of hops, developed by HRI using 'good parental breeding', which grow to half the height of conventional hops (2.4 metres) and which are less prone to pest attack. Also known as low trellis hops.

Earl Soham Brewery Suffolk village brewery since 1984.

early doors northern expression for opening time (often heard in Lancashire).

East Kent Goldings a cask-conditioned organic beer brewed by Pitfield (London).

East Kent Goldings a British aroma hop with an alpha acid content of 5-6%. The resulting aroma is spicy, floral.

eau *(French)* water.

EBC *(abbreviation)* European Brewing Convention scale: European standard measurement of the colour range of a specific beer or beer style. The darker the malt, the higher its EBC value. See SRM. Conversion calculations: EBC = SRM x 1.97. SRM = EBC / 1.97.

EBCU *(abbreviation)* The European Beer Consumers' Union. It was formed to fight the consumer cause regarding brewery ownership, labelling information etc. at EU and international level.

EBU *(abbreviation)* European Bittering Units: the standard method of measuring the amount of bitterness in a given volume of beer.

Eccleshall Brewery brewery, opened in 1995 in outbuildings behind the George Hotel, Stafford.

Eco Warrior a cask-conditioned organic beer brewed by Pitfield (London).

economiser an old style of beer engine: a pipe connecting a beer engine drip-trap to the top of the pump. The beer overflowing the glass into the drip tray is re-cycled through the pump. Also known as an Autovac.

effervescence the bubbles or fizz in beer. The amount depends on the amount of dissolved carbon dioxide.

Eggenberg an Austrian triple bock.

Eggenberg an Austrian smoke beer.

80/-ale Scottish term for premium beers; see Shilling System. Usually 1040-1050 and light in colour. Sometimes referred to as 'Export'.

Einbeck the original home of German Bock beer, near Hannover, with just one remaining brewery (owned by DUB-Schultheiss) producing the classic Einbecker Ur-Bock.

Eisbock *(German: "ice" bock)* the strongest type of German Doppelbock, with an amazing alcohol content of over 12 per cent. It is made by partly freezing the beer and then, since water freezes before alcohol, removing the ice to concentrate this very rich beer. The leading example is Kulminator.

EKU *(abbreviation; German)* Erste Kulmbacher Brewery of Bavaria. It is famed for its Eisbock, Kulminator

28 Urtyp Hell, one of the strongest regularly-produced beers in the world.

Eldridge Pope Dorset brewery, which is part of the Thomas Hardy brewing business.

electric pump electrical device to deliver the beer from a cask to the counter dispenser. There are two main types of electric pump: free flow and metered positive displacement. Free flow pumps are of the impeller type: they are switched on by a pressure switch that senses a drop in beer line pressure when the tap is opened, and they continue to run until closing the tap causes a pressure pulse that resets the pressure switch. The displacement type pump has a calibrated half-pint container from which the beer is displaced whenever a push-button at the dispense point is pressed. Displacement metered pumps are measured and sealed by the Customs & Excise and consequently they may be used with unmarked glasses, unlike any other dispense method.

Elephant Carlsberg's Danish export lager, named after the stone elephants at the Copenhagen brewery gate.

Elgood & Sons Ltd. Fenland riverside brewery known as "Elgood's" and brewing at the Georgian North Brink Brewery in Wisbech, Cambridgeshire.

embouteillée par *(French)* bottled by.

Emerson Brewing Company established 1993 in Dunedin, New Zealand. Winner of several Australasian awards.

EMP pathway *(brewing)* the sequence of metabolic reactions in cells which hydrolyse carbohydrate.

en bouteille *(French)* in a bottle.

endosperm the tissue within the barley grain which contains starch and protein.

enterobacteriaceae enteric bacteria: lambic bacteria strains, occurring naturally in the Brabant area of Belgium.

Entire an early form of porter, properly called 'entire butts' to indicate that it was brewed to reproduce in one beer (and hence entirely in one cask or butt) the characteristics of three separate beers (pale ale, brown ale, and stock ale) sold in the early 18th century as 'three threads' or 'three thirds'. Each of the three beers was tapped in turn into the pot to give a mixture; this obviously required more time than if the beer was drawn from one cask, and hence in 1722 Ralph Harwood, a brewer in Shoreditch, hit on the idea of replacing 'three threads' with 'entire butts'.

Enville Ales Stourbridge brewery on a picturesque Victorian farm complex.

enzyme complex protein, which increases the rate of a chemical reaction on one specific substrate. Enzymes are sensitive to heat and have a low tolerance to acid solutions with a pH of 4 and less. To satisfy CAMRA's definition of a pure beer, enzymes should not be added.

épices *(French)* spices.

Epsom salts magnesium sulphate, a compound used to harden water.

Erdinger a Bavarian wheat beer.

Eroica an American general purpose/bittering hop.

Erste Kulmbacher Bavarian brewery famous for its strong Eisbock – Kulminator 28 Urtyp Hell. Abbreviation: EKU.

eskie Australian term for a portable thermos case used for keeping beer cool.

essential oils the volatile oils in hops, which retain the flavour and odour of the hops when extracted.

estate inns alehouses provided for their workers by wealthy landowners.

esters organic compounds produced from an acid and an alcohol which are produced during fermentation. Many have powerful fruity aromas. The fermentation process and the type of yeast used effect the production of esters.

estery *(beer evaluation)* having a fruity (typically banana or pear) or bubble-gum aftertaste, often a characteristic of ale yeast. Levels are enhanced by high fermentation temperatures.

ethanol ethyl alcohol or spirits of wine; the colourless and odourless active content of alcoholic drinks.

ethylaldehyde alternative term for acetaldehyde: a volatile liquid resulting from the breakdown of sugars during fermentation.

European Beer Consumers' Union formed to fight the consumer cause regarding brewery ownership, labelling information etc. at EU and international level. Abbreviation: EBCU.

European Bittering Units the standard method of measuring the amount of bitterness in a given volume of beer. Abbreviation: EBU.

European Brewing Convention scale European standard measurement of the colour range of a specific beer or beer style. Abbreviation: EBC. The darker the malt, the higher its EBC value. The colour of the beer does not just depend on the type of malt, but also on the brewing conditions. See also SRM.

Everards Brewery Ltd. independent family-owned brewery on the outskirts of Leicester, run by the great, great grandson of the founder.

Evesham Brewery set up in 1992, this former bottle store at The Green Dragon Inn has become a thriving tourist attraction.

Ex-Beer alcohol-free lager from the Swiss Feldschlosschen brewery.

excise the tax levied by the Customs and Excise department on all of the beer that a brewer produces. CAMRA supports a complete revision of the excise duty payable on alcoholic drinks and seeks a two-thirds reduction in the current excise duty on beer. High levels of excise duty cause encomic and social problems as pubs and breweries are undermined by cheap imported beer. CAMRA believes the duty should be reduced to a level that removes the incentive to smuggle. Smuggled beer threatens attempts to tackle alcoholism and underage drinking. See bootleg lager.

Exe Valley Brewery Devonshire brewery using spring water, Devon malt and English hops. Called Exe since 1991 when it expanded from Barron's Brewery (established 1984).

Exmoor Ales Ltd. Somerset's largest brewery founded in 1980.

Experimental a US aroma hop for German-style lagers.

export term applied to premium beers that may or may not be exported. Name often interchangeable with IPA (India Pale Ale). In Scotland, export may be keg brews or cask 80/- ales.

extract hop extract; glutinous liquid comprising the essential substances from hops. Available in cans for use in homebrew kits.

extract malt extract; syrup obtained from an infusion of malt. Available in cans for use in homebrew kits. The extract should be derived from 100% barley malt to satisfy CAMRA's definition of pure beer.

extractor a piece of equipment designed to remove or separate e.g. CO_2.

°F *(abbreviation)* Fahrenheit, measured according to the Fahrenheit scale.

fadøl *(Danish)* draft beer.

Fahrenheit scale a scale of temperatures in which 32°F represents the melting point of ice and 212°F represents the boiling point of water.

Falcon Ales Okell's beers from the Isle of Man.

Falstaff Brewery Derby small-scale enterprise.

Family Ale an old name for light bitter beer, usually bottled.

Farmers Arms Gloucestershire brewery started in 1993 and purchased by Wadworth in 1997.

Far North Brewery Scottish "very micro" brewery, supplying cask ale to the nuclear site at Dounreay.

Faro a draught Belgian lambic beer, with sugar added.

Farsons Malta's sole brewery (full name Simonds Farsons Cisk) which, thanks to the island's former British connections, brews the only top-fermented ales in the Mediterranean, although all are pasteurised.

Fat God's Brewery brewery installed in 1997 next to the Queen's Head pub in Evesham.

Faxe *(Danish: "draught")* Danish brewery producing unpasteurised beer.

Faxe Fad a Danish bottled lager (4.5 per cent alcohol).

Featherstone Brewery Leicestershire company which specialises in customised, personalised beers.

Federation Clubs brewery in Newcastle, popularly known as 'Fed'.

Felinfoel Brewery Co. family-owned brewery and the oldest in Wales, based in Llanelli.

Fenland Brewery established in Chatteris, Cambridgeshire in 1997.

fermentable able to undergo fermentation.

fermentation *(brewing)* biochemical reaction when sugar is converted to ethyl alcohol by yeast and some bacteria i.e. the stage when yeast is added to the fermentation vessels to convert the wort into beer.

fermentation basse *(French)* bottom-fermented.

fermentation en bouteille *(French)* bottle-fermented.

fermentation haute *(French)* top-fermented.

fermentation lock *(brewing)* a one-way valve which allows excess carbon dioxide to be expelled during fermentation, whilst preventing contaminants from entering the fermenting vessel. Also known as air lock.

fermentation spontanée *(French)* spontaneous fermentation.

fermenter *(brewing)* a vessel used to contain wort during fermentation.

Fernandes Brewery Wakefield concern since 1997. It incorporates a home-brew shop and specialist beer off-licence.

Fiddlers Ales Ltd. Nottinghamshire brewery supplying locals since 1996.

Figgy Sue diluted beer simmered with dried figs and ginger and drunk hot.

Fighting Fund *(Campaign)* The Real Ale Fighting Fund – a specific fund for raising awareness of real ale through the 'Ask if it's Cask' campaign. Members and branches organise raffles, competitions and other fund-raising activities in addition to their normal campaigning.

filter (to) *(brewing)* to extract solids from a beer.

filtered beer a beer from which the solids (yeast) have been extracted. CAMRA believes that the practice of filtering beer and then re-seeding it and selling it as cask-conditioned real ale is unacceptable unless there is sufficient live yeast and fermentable material in the cask to ensure a satisfactory secondary fermentation.

final attenuation *(brewing)* the final degree of attenuation.

final degree of attenuation *(brewing)* the maximum apparent attenuation which can be attained by a wort. Formula: final degree of attenuation = (OG in °B – final gravity in °B) x 100.

final gravity the British brewing industry's method of expressing the strength of beer as measured when all fermentable sugars have been converted to alcohol and carbon dioxide. See original gravity.

final specific gravity the final gravity.

fine (to) *(brewing)* to add finings to a cask or vessel.

finings a glutinous syrup made from the swim bladder of the sturgeon fish found in the South China Sea. Several pints of 'finings' are added to each cask of traditional beer to precipitate the yeast cells, leaving the beer 'bright'. Also known as isinglass and copper finings.

finish *(beer evaluation)* term for the aesthetic appeal of a beer. See polish. Also a term referring to the aftertaste.

finished beer beer which has undergone fermentation and aging and is ready to be racked. The term does not apply to wort or beer which is still undergoing fermentation.

finishing hops hops added to the wort late in the boil to impart a hoppy aroma rather than bitterness.

fir tree   the part of the spigot of a tail, grooved to grip the inside of the pipe.

firkin   a 9-gallon cask. The name derives from Middle Dutch 'vierdek-ijn' (fourth part of a barrel).

Firkin   the common name of a chain of homebrew pubs in London, e.g. Goose & Firkin and Fox & Firkin.

First Gold a British dwarf aroma hop variety, introduced commercially in the mid 1990s, with an alpha acid content of 7-8%.

First In Last Out Brewery (Filo)
Hastings brewery since 1985, brewing Crofters and Cardinal.

fish gelatine alternative term for isinglass.

Fisherrow Brewery   Edinburgh concern launched in 1999 on a council-owned industrial unit.

Fix   Greece's best-known lager.

flagon   a quart bottle. The original takeaway container.

Flagship Brewery Chatham brewery housed in the town's historic dockyard since 1995.

flaked barley an adjunct used particularly in mild ales.

flaked maize an adjunct used particularly in mild ales.

flaked wheat an adjunct used particularly in mild ales.

Flannery's Brewery   A b e r y s t w y t h pub-based brewery since 1997.

Flasche   *(German)* bottle.

Flaschengärung   *(German)* bottle-fermented.

flash cooler small refrigeration unit connected directly to the drink supply line near to the dispense tap, thus serving the drink at the required temperature without having to cool the bulk container. Flash coolers should never be used with cask-conditioned beers.

flaske   *(Danish)* bottle.

flaskeøl   *(Danish)* bottled beer.

flat   *(beer evaluation)* having lost effervescence.

flavour wheel   *(beer evaluation)* a list of beer evaluation terminology prepared by the American Society of Brewing Chemists, the European Brewery Convention and the Master Brewers' Association of America to standardise descriptions of beer flavours.

flavoured ale beers and ales to which herbs, spices and/or other flavourings have been added.

flavoursome *(beer evaluation)* being full of flavour.

fles   *(Dutch)* bottle.

flocculation *(brewing)* beer and/or wort clarifying process during which the finings or other clarifying agents (see carragheen) cause proteinaceous particles or yeast cells to clump together into fluffy lumps which can then fall out of suspension.

flogger   a flat wooden tool used to cork a bottle. See crown cap.

flooring   see floor maltings.

floor maltings *(malting)* the most traditional method of turning barley into malt. During germination barley is evenly spread on a malting floor to a depth of around 20cm and is turned over (often manually) to dispel excess heat and allow even respiration and germination.

floral *(beer evaluation)* having a taste or aroma associated with flowers (typically rose or hyacinth) determined by the type of hops used.

flower   alternative term for the hop cone.

Flowers   famous British brewing name resurrected by Whitbread for some of their southern beers, chiefly brewed at Cheltenham, and for their West Midlands trading company. The original brewery at Stratford-upon-Avon was closed in 1968.

foam a description of the bubbles on the top of a glass of beer. See head.

fob   excessive and troublesome froth often seen when lager or keg beers are served; in which case the cause is over carbonation. Fobbing can occur with Real Ale if there is an air leak in the connections to the cask.

Forge Brewery   Hastings brewery established in 1995. Acquired Pett Brewing Company in 1998.

Forshaw   old brewing name now used by Burtonwood.

Forth Brewery Co. Alloa brewing company set up by former Maclay head brewer Duncan Kellock in 1999.

four sheets to the wind   *(slang)* description of someone who is drunk.

four-vessel system *(homebrewing)* standard brewing equipment for lager-style beers: mash tun, mash cooker, lauter tun, kettle.

framboise   a Belgian Gueuze beer in which the second fermentation has been caused by adding raspberries.

framboos   raspberry lambic.

frambozen   raspberry lambic.

Frankenstein beer a negative reference to beers of the future, which could be brewed using genetically modified ingredients.

Franklin's Brewery   Harrogate brewery set up in 1980.

Frankton Bagby   an independent brewery established in Rugby in 1999 by three local families.

Freedom Brewing Company Ltd.
opened in 1995 as the first dedicated lager micro-brewer in Britain.

free flow an impeller-type electric pump which delivers a keg or top pressure beer to the counter dispenser. The pressurised keg is connected directly to a small on-off tap. The beer flows freely as long as the tap is held open.

Free House a pub supposedly free of any brewery tie, and therefore able to offer a range of beers from different breweries. Term often abused nowadays. CAMRA believes that the term 'Free House' should be confined to premises which are at liberty to sell the products of any brewery company and believes that this should be supported by appropriate legislation.

Freeminer Brewery Ltd. Coleford brewery, established in 1992 and located in the Royal Forest of Dean in Gloucestershire.

frigo *(Dutch; "cold")* fridge temperature.

Frog Island Brewery Northampton brewery started in 1994, specialising in personalised beer bottles, available by mail order.

froment *(French)* wheat.

Fromes Hill Brewery brewery in Herefordshire, founded in 1993.

Frome Valley Brewery Herefordshire brewery founded in 1997 and established in a former 18th Century hop kiln.

froth the bubbles on the top of a glass, more often known as the head. See head.

frothblowers pub-goers in the 1930s, who organised themselves into the informal Ancient Order of Frothblowers, mixing social activities with the collection of large sums for children's charities.

fructose *(brewing)* a form of easily fermentable sugar used in brewing as an adjunct or for priming. Formula: $C_6H_{12}O_6$.

Früh (Kölner Hofbrau) famous German homebrew house opposite Cologne Cathedral, serving a fine example of the city's own beer, Kölsch, which is now brewed off the premises.

fruit machine an electronic gambling machine in a pub giving cash prizes, known in the trade as AWP (amusements with prizes). CAMRA is concerned that these noisy electronic amusement machines have a damaging effect on the traditional character of many pubs.

fruity *(beer evaluation)* having a citrus flavour (typically orange or grapefruit).

Fuggles an American aroma hop with a 4.5-5% alpha acid content, used primarily in dark beers and stouts.

full pint campaign *(Campaign)* a CAMRA call for a fair deal on pub measures. CAMRA supports the retention of the pint measure for draught beers and believes that appropriate Weights & Measures legislation should exist which defines a pint of beer as 20fl oz of liquid excluding any head of froth or foam. CAMRA undertakes a full pints survey to demonstrate that lined glasses and/or measured dispense will not mean higher prices for customers.

Fuller, Smith and Turner PLC Fuller's Griffin Brewery in Chiswick is London's oldest. It supplies Fuller's own pubs and the free trade. Fuller's refers to the brewery or a beer from the brewery, as in "a pint of Fuller's".

fully mashed beers *(brewing)* beers produced from mash brewing, a brewing method which extracts fermentable sugars from crushed malted barley grain (as opposed to using malt extract).

fun pub a phenomenon of the 1980s, where the music was deemed to be louder, the lights brighter, and the customers more youthful than at the pub down the road.

Fyfe Brewing Company b a s e d behind the Harbour Bar since 1995.

GABF *(abbreviation)* Great American Beer Festival: an annual festival run by the American Brewers' Association.

gær *(Danish)* yeast.

gæret i flaske *(Danish)* bottle fermented.

gæret øl *(Danish)* beer with yeast sediment i.e. unfiltered.

Galena an American bittering hop variety with an alpha acid content of 13-14%.

Gale's see George Gale & Co.

gallon the basis of the Imperial system of liquid measure. A gallon is the volume of 10lbs of distilled water. A gallon is eight pints, the metric equivalent is 4.54 litres. The US gallon is four-fifths of the British one. 'Play for the gallon' is an expression in pub games where each losing team member has to buy a drink for his opponent.

Gambrinus a Czech Pilsner.

Gambrinus France national organisation for collectors of breweriana in France.

garnet *(beer evaluation)* a colour definition.

gassy *(beer evaluation)* having too much dissolved carbon dioxide.

Gasthof *(German)* pub/restaurant.

Gaststätte *(German)* pub/restaurant.

GBBF *(abbreviation; Campaign)* Great British Beer Festival: an annual celebration of traditional British beers run by unpaid CAMRA volunteers, who man the biggest bar in the world for a week, serving hundreds of different real ales. This national festival is held in London, Olympia in August every year. There is also entertainment, food and an excellent family room. Abbreviation: GBBF.

gebotteld door *(Dutch)* bottled by.

gebraut von *(German)* brewed by.

gebrouwen door *(Dutch)* brewed by.

gelatine a glutinous substance derived from animal hooves which is used as a fining agent.

gelatinisation *(brewing)* the enzymic process by which alph-amylase degrades starch into soluble polysaccharides. Also called liquefaction.

general purpose hops hybrid varieties of disease-resistant hops which have high yields and a moderate alpha acid content. They can be used as both bittering or aroma hops.

Genesee the main producers of American Cream Ale (4.75 per cent alcohol), from Rochester, New York. The company also brews a stronger ale called Twelve Horse.

genetically modified applying to an organism whose characteristics have been altered by the insertion of genes from another organism into its DNA. See Frankenstein beer. Abbreviation: GM.

George Bateman & Son Ltd.
Wainfleet brewery which started brewing in 1874 for local farmers. A family firm with award-winning beers.

George Gale & Co. Gale's is a Hampshire brewery dating from the mid 1800s.

germinate (to) *(malting)* to sprout seeds or spores or to cause seeds or spores to sprout.

germinating floor *(malting)* floor maltings.

germination *(malting)* the second stage in the beermaking process, in which the steeped barley grains are drained and left to sprout for several days. Germination can be triggered or accelerated by spraying the steeped barley with gibberellic acid.

germination boxes *(malting)* Saladin boxes: huge, uncovered, open-ended, rectangular boxes used for modifying barley during the malting process.

gerst *(Dutch)* barley.

Gerste *(German)* barley.

Ghilde des Eswards Cervoisiers *(French)* a wing of the French organisation Les Amis de la Bière.

gibberellic acid *(brewing)* a natural acid added to the steeping water in order to encourage embryo development in the malting process.

Gibb's Mew defunct Salisbury brewery, fondly remembered for its dark, strong Bishop's Tipple.

gill a quarter of a pint. Most frequently used to indicate spirit measures. The 'optics' in England are generally a sixth of a gill, and in Scotland a fifth.

gill term used for a half pint of beer in Lancashire and Yorkshire.

gill *(slang)* any drink, as in 'let's go for a gill'.

gin palace a style of pub whose origins coincide with the popularity of gin in the 19th century, consequent upon a reduction in duty on spirits. Flamboyant and often gaudy in style, rich in ornament and decoration; a contrast with the (then) squalid public house.

gist *(Dutch/Flemish)* yeast.

Glas *(Dutch/German)* glass.

glass a half pint (used especially in Ireland).

glucose *(brewing)* a form of easily fermentable sugar used in brewing as an adjunct or for priming. Formula: $C_6H_{12}O_6$. See also dextrose.

glycolysis *(brewing)* the breaking down of starches to sugar by enzymes during fermentation.

glycoprotein a protein derivative of barley.

Goacher's see P & DJ Goacher.

Goddards Brewery Isle of Wight farm-based brewery near Ryde since 1993.

Goffs Brewery Gloucestershire family concern since 1994.

Golden Promise a strain of barley, grown in Scotland, used for ale malt.

Golden Promise an organic beer brewed by the Caledonian Brewery in Edinburgh, available in cask-conditioned as well as bottled form.

Goldfinch Brewery brewing since 1987 at rear of Tom Brown's public house in Dorchester.

Goldings a traditional variety of aroma hop with a 5.3 alpha acid content.

Good Beer Guide *(Campaign)* the UK's leading guide to pubs and 'real ale' beers, published annually in early October. Pubs are only listed if they serve outstanding real ale. This is assessed by local CAMRA branch members who survey the pubs in their area. The first Good Beer Guide was published by CAMRA in 1974 and the original edition was withdrawn because of fear of prosecution over the comment on Watney's beers "Avoid like the plague".

good parental breeding a development pioneered by the Horticultural Research International at Wye which involves taking disease-resistant genes from current hop varieties to develop new varieties.

goods *(brewing)* the contents of the mash tun – malt plus any other grains or adjuncts.

Goose Eye Brewery small Yorkshire concern re-established in 1991.

Gose a traditional top-fermented light white beer from barley, wheat and oat malt, which have not been oast dried. Few hops but salt and herbs are added. The river Gose, which flows through Goslar, where this beer was first brewed gives it its name.

Goudenband Speciaal Provisie a bottle-conditioned ale from Liefmans of Belgium, (6.5 per cent alcohol). There are also a commoner Oudenaarde Speciaal (5.25) and a cherry Kriek (7.5), both based on Provisie.

government stamped any glass used in a pub for draught beer or cider must be government stamped i.e. it has to have been tested by the

Customs and Excise and must bear the tester's mark – the crown and a number.

grain bed *(brewing)* the solid particles and grain husks on top of the false bottom of the lauter tun, which act as a filter during sparging.

grains *(brewing)* spent goods.

Grainstore Brewery brews in Rutland for Davises Brewing Company.

grainy *(beer evaluation)* having a husk or cereal aftertaste.

Grand Cru the premium version of the unique Belgian white beer, Hoegaards Wit, with an alcohol content of 7.5 per cent.

grande *(Italian: "large")* a standard 'large' glass of beer.

Grandma a mixed pint, either old and mild or else (Midlands) sweet stout and old.

grant *(brewing)* the sink for the outflow of the lauter tun.

grassy *(beer evaluation)* having a grass-like or crushed vegetation aftertaste, sometimes resulting from the grain having been stored in warm and humid conditions.

gravity a method of serving beer direct from a cask behind the bar.

gravity a measure of the density of beer. See original gravity.

gravity units the final gravity expressed as a whole number e.g. final gravity 1.025 = 25 gravity units.

Great American Beer Festival annual festival run by the American Brewers' Association. Abbreviation: GABF.

Great British Beer Festival *(Campaign)* an annual celebration of traditional British beers run by unpaid CAMRA volunteers, who man the biggest bar in the world for a week, serving hundreds of different real ales. This national festival is held in London, Olympia in August every year. There is also entertainment, food and an excellent family room. Abbreviation: GBBF.

green beer a term applied to beer brewed using organic ingredients. See organic beer.

green beer young beer at the end of primary fermentation or beer that has not had long enough to mature in the cask; such beer has a harsh, rough palate. Unfortunately, economic pressures are tempting brewers and licensees to sell ever younger beer.

Green Bullet a New Zealand general purpose hop with an alpha acid content of 11-12%.

Green Dragon free house and brewery in Bungay, Suffolk. Brewing since 1991.

Green Jack Brewing Co. started in 1993 on the old Forbes Brewery site in Lowestoft.

green malt *(malting)* term applied to barley after modification and prior to kilning.

Green Tye Brewery Hertfordshire producer since 1999.

Greene King PLC Bury St Edmunds independent founded in 1799 and now an East Anglian giant. Acquired Morland and Ruddles, closing their breweries.

Gribble Brewery microbrewery owned by Badger.

Grimbergen an Abbaye-style beer from the Maes brewery of Belgium.

grist *(brewing)* milled ('cracked') malt and adjuncts before mashing. Malted barley, the main ingredient of the mash, has to be milled ('cracked') into a coarse powder to allow the fermentable materials to be extracted.

grist case *(brewing)* a large hopper that contains the 'cracked' malt (grist). In a traditional tower brewery the grist case is on the upper floor above the mash tun into which the grist is dropped.

grits uncooked, milled cereals, used predominantly by American and Australian breweries.

grog Australian term for alcoholic beverage.

grog blossom *(slang)* term for a heavy drinker's red nose.

Grolsch Dutch brewery from Groenlo, internationally renowned for its distinctive pot-stoppered, embossed bottle. The Pilsener inside is equally traditional, being unpasteurised and conditioned for two months.

Grosvenor a tall fount: a tall pillar-tap mounting stationed on a bar, used to dispense traditional beers in Scotland.

Grünhalle *(German: "green hall")* lager 'brewed the Bavarian way', devised by Edward Greenall, Chairman of Randalls Vautier of Jersey.

GU *(abbreviation)* gravity units: the final gravity expressed as a whole number e.g. final gravity 1.025 = 25 gravity units.

Guernsey Brewery Co. set in the harbour of St. Peter Port, this Channel Island brewery has a history dating back to 1856.

guest ales *(Campaign)* a campaigning initiative to win pub tenants the right to satisfy the wishes of their own customers by stocking guest ales.

guest beer *(Campaign)* a beer, not regularly sold in a pub, being on offer for a limited period. CAMRA supports legislation to allow both tenanted and managed pubs of the national brewers to choose a cask-conditioned guest beer of the licensees' own choice.

guest beer rights *(Campaign)*   the Guest Beer provision was introduced into law in 1990, giving Britain's small brewers access to the tenanted and leased pubs of the National brewers. A CAMRA campaign landmark.

Gueuze   a blend of wild Lambic beers from Belgium which ferment again to form a stronger, fruitier brew (5.5 per cent alcohol), sometimes conditioned for years. Good examples include Lindemans and Timmermans. The most commercial is Belle Vue.

Guinness world-famous Irish stout brewers, which has world-wide brewing operations and distribution. Arthur Guinness bought the Rainsford brewery in 1759 and brewed porter that became "Extra Stout Porter". By 1838 the historic Guinness Brewery had become the largest in Ireland. Annual production had risen to one million barrels in 1881 and by 1914 the brewery was the biggest in the world.

Guinness Hopstore   the Guinness visitors' centre in Dublin.

Gulløl   *(Norwegian)* Golden "export lager" (max. 7.0% ABV).

gush excessive and troublesome froth often seen when lager or keg beers are served; in which case the cause

is over carbonation. Gush can occur with Real Ale if there is an air leak in the connections to the cask.

gushing beer wild beer.

gyle *(brewing)* the batch of beer from one brewing. Casks are usually identified with a 'gyle number' or date code.

gyle worting *(brewing)* see gyling.

gyling   *(brewing)* the act of priming with actively fermenting wort rather than sugars. See also kräusening.

gypsum   hydrated calcium sulphate – the chief mineral constituent of hard water. It is ideal for making bitter beers. Formula: $CaSO_4.2H_2O$. See Burtonise.

Hacker-Pschorr German brewery in Munich.

Hacker-Pschorr a German lager.

Hacker-Pschorr a German March beer.

Hafnia protea bacteria which convert nitrate into nitrite, which inhibits yeast metabolism.

Haggards Brewery Ltd. Chelsea-based concern.

Hairoun brewery on the Caribbean island of St. Vincent, brewing a range of German-style lagers.

Halcyon a type of malt

Hale & Hearty Brewery Surrey business established in 1996.

half a half pint measure of beer, ale etc.

half a measure of whisky/whiskey in Scotland or Ireland. So don't ask for this if you're expecting a half-pint of beer!

half-and-half an equal mixture of two beers in a pint, usually mild and bitter.

Hall & Woodhouse Dorset family brewery since 1777, known for its 'Badger Beers'. Now trading as Badger.

Hall's former Oxford brewery which ceased brewing in 1952. The name was revived in 1980 to cover Allied's West Country pubs.

Hallertauer a New Zealand general purpose/bittering hop with an alpha acid content of 9-10%.

Hallertauer Hersbrucker a German aroma hop variety with an alpha acid content of 3.5-4.5%. The resulting aroma is spicy, earthy.

Hallertauer Mittelfrüh the most famous German aroma hop variety from Bavaria with an alpha acid content of 5-5.5%.

Hambleton Ales growing brewery established in 1991 in Vale of York.

hammered *(slang)* description of someone who is drunk.

Hampshire Brewery set up in 1992; grew into a larger site in Romsey.

Hanby Ales Shropshire brewery set up in 1990.

Hancock Cardiff brewery taken over by Bass in 1968 and operated as Welsh Brewers, retaining some Hancock beers. Sold to Brains in 1999.

handle a glass mug with a handle.

handpull the operating handle of a beer engine.

handpump the more usual name for the beer engine, since it is the part customers see in the bar; also sometimes known as a handpull. The sign of Real Ale.

Hannen most widely available brand of Alt, the German dark ale, produced at three breweries around Düsseldorf with an alcohol content of 4.5 per cent.

Hansa German brewery, part of the DAB group in Dortmund, Germany.

Hanson's part of the Wolverhampton and Dudley Breweries since the forties, the brewery was closed in 1991 but name lived on in Hanson's Mild and in pub liveries.

happy day Scottish term for a pint, made up of 2/3 pt of Light or 60/- ale together with a 'wee heavy' – a nip-sized bottle of barley wine.

hard spile a wooden peg made from close-grained timber, which is inserted in the shive to control the carbon dioxide content of the beer.

Hardys & Hanson Nottingham family brewery, the result of a merger in 1930 between two neighbouring firms in Kimberley.

harsh *(beer evaluation)* astringent.

Hart Brewery Lancashire brewery founded in 1994.

Hartleys former Cumbrian brewery at Ulverston famous for its 'Beers from the Wood', taken over by Robinsons of Stockport in 1982. Closed in 1991. Hartley's XB is still produced.

Harvey & Son established in 1790 in Lewes, Sussex. The Bridge Wharf Brewery, on the banks of the River Ouse, has been effected by floods.

Harviestoun Brewery Ltd. established in 1985 in a Clackmannanshire dairy.

haver *(Dutch)* oats.

hazardous levels alcohol consumption which exceeds the safe limits: generally defined as between 21 and 49 units a week for men and between 14 and 35 units a week for women.

haze a lack of clarity in beer; a milkiness in which no actual particles can be seen. See chill.

hazy *(beer evaluation)* slightly cloudy, due to suspended microorganisms or protein precipitates.

HB *(abbreviation)* Hofbrauhaus: the state-owned former royal brewery of Bavaria, which, besides its famous Munich beer hall, developed German Bock beer. Its Maibock is a classic of its style. HB also popularised Weizenbier (wheat beer) in South Germany, producing an excellent Edel-Weizen ('noble wheat').

HB Clark Co (Successors) Ltd. Clark's resumed cask ale production in 1982 at their Westgate brewery in Wakefield.

HBU *(abbreviation)* hop bitterness unit.

head the cask end. The front head holds the keystone.

head the froth on the top of a glass of beer. Drinkers in some areas consider the nature of the head to be almost as important as the quality of the beer itself. A tight head is obtained by forcing the beer through very small orifices in the sparkler on the pump, making a stiff creamy foam of almost invisibly small bubbles. The beer is drunk 'through' the head. In most of the north of England and Scotland beer is served with a large head, whilst most of the southern area prefers the loose head – a light froth of large irregular bubbles which rapidly collapse.

head brewer the senior brewer in a brewery, frequently now called production manager or director.

headspace the space between the surface of the liquid and the top of the container.

heat exchange unit *(brewing)* a wort cooler.

heating jackets *(brewing)* a modification of steam coils by which 'jackets' are fitted to the side of a copper and steam pumped into them to boil the wort. The term can also be used for any 'jacket' fitted to a tank.

Heather Ale Ltd. operates out of the Craigmill Brewery in Lanarkshire.

heavy Scottish term for medium gravity beer, usually 1034-39. Otherwise known as 70/- ale. Confusingly, 'heavy' is usually light in colour, whereas 'light' is dark. Do not confuse with 'wee heavy', a nip of Scottish barley wine.

heavy drinker a person who regularly consumes more than six units of alcohol a day (i.e. exceeds the safe levels). See hazardous; safe levels.

heel taps any dregs left in a nominally empty glass. The term possibly derives from the same expression used for the small segment of leather used to mend a shoe heel.

Hefe *(German)* yeast. Mit Hefe: with yeast.

hefefrei *(German: "without yeast")* filtered.

hefetrüb *(German)* description of wheat beer with yeast particles.

Hefeweissbier *(German)* a wheat beer containing yeast.

Hefeweizen *(German)* see Hefeweissbier.

Heineken one of the world's largest brewers and most famous brands.

hell *(German)* pale or light.

Heller a German Kölsch.

Henninger internationally-known Frankfurt brewery, whose bottled Henninger Pils (1044) has been imported into Britain by Courage.

Henstridge Brewery Somerset single beer brewer since 1994.

Herald Northern Ireland's second small free trade brewery, set up in Coleraine in 1983, though the cask beer, Herald Ale (1036), is usually sold under blanket pressure.

herb *(German)* dry.

hergist in de fles *(Flemish)* bottle-fermented.

Hesket Newmarket Brewery Ltd. brewery set up in 1988 in an attractive North Lakes village.

Hexhamshire Brewery Northumberland family brewery since 1992.

HG Wells Planets Brewery opened in 1996 in a leisure complex in Woking.

high alpha hops bittering hops. High alpha refers to the percentage of alpha acid present in the alpha resin: high = 8 to 12%.

High Force Hotel and Brewery founded in 1995, claiming to be the highest in Britain at 1,060 feet.

high gravity brewing *(brewing)* a modern development aimed at economising on brewery plant and material handling costs. Very strong beer is brewed and this is then diluted to the desired gravity after filtration. The practice is now almost universal with big commercial brewers although not often used with cask beer.

higher alcohols *(beer evaluation)* solvent-tasting alcohols, often produced by high temperature fermentation. (One cause of hangovers).

Highgate & Walsall Brewing Company now a subsidiary of Aston Manor after chequered past. The brewery celebrated its centenary in 1998 and some of the original Victorian equipment is still in use.

Highwood Brewery Ltd. Lincolnshire brewery started in 1995.

Higsons a former independent brewery in Liverpool.

Hilden Brewing Company pioneer brewery of real ale in Northern Ireland, when the brewery was set up in Lisburn, near Belfast, in 1981.

Hirschgarten a beer garden in Munich, Bavaria, which can seat several thousand people.

Hite a Korean lager.

Hobsons Brewery & Co. Worcestershire-based brewery, established in 1993.

Hoegaarden a cloudy, yellow-white Belgian beer, brewed from raw wheat and malted barley.

Hoegaarden multinational beer corporation in Belgium, producing primarily white beer.

Hofbrauhaus the state-owned former royal brewery of Bavaria, which, besides its famous Munich beer hall, developed German Bock beer. Its Maibock is a classic of its style. The brewery also popularised Weizenbier (wheat beer) in South Germany, producing an excellent Edel-Weizen ('noble wheat'). Abbreviation: HB.

hoge gisting *(Dutch/Flemish)* top-fermented.

Hogs Back Brewery purpose-built brewery in 18th-century farm building in Surrey since 1992.

hogshead a 54-gallon cask, now fairly uncommon although some northern brewers still use them. A full wooden hogshead weighs more than a third of a ton!

Holdens Brewery Limited family brewery of the Black Country at Woodsetton, near Dudley, going back four generations.

Holsten company in North Germany, with breweries in several cities. Known in Britain for its bottled Diat Pils (1045), a strong dry lager from Hamburg. Another notable product is Moravia Pils.

holy ales the collective term for ales brewed in the abbeys of Belgium (Chimay, Orval, Rochefort, Westmalle, Westvleteren) and the Netherlands (Schaapskooi), which operate or license commercial breweries.

Holt Manchester brewery that celebrated 150 years of brewing in 1999. All the company's pubs serve real ale and deliveries are made in 54-gallon hogsheads. Brewery tours are available.

Home former Nottingham brewery.

Home County Brewers Gloucestershire brewery set up in 1997.

homebrew (to) to brew beer at home for private consumption.

homebrew beer brewed at home by an amateur.

homebrew house a pub which brews its own ale. Up to the beginning of this century, these were commonplace, but by the early 1970s only four survived. However, the real ale boom has encouraged licensees and major breweries alike to install small homebrew plants in pubs.

homemade beer homebrew beer.

Honey Dew a cask-conditioned organic beer brewed by Fuller's.

honey wine mead.

honeyed ale a Belgian ale to which honey has been added, not just as a sugar for fermentation, but to impart flavour.

Hook Norton Brewery Co. since 1849 this Oxfordshire brewery near Banbury has made beers with water drawn from the wells beneath. It is probably the best remaining example in Britain of a Victorian tower brewery.

hoop the metal band around a wooden cask.

hop a perennial plant from the Cannabaceae family – a group that includes both the nettle and cannabis. The brewers' hop, Humulus lupulus, grows as a climbing vine (always clockwise) trained along frameworks of poles and wire. The harvested plant is the flower head. The flowers carry minute granules of yellow resin, lupulin, which contain the aromatic compounds that give the hop its bittering and preserving power. The main bitter agent is alpha acid. Before use by the brewer, hops are dried and packed into large sacks, called pockets. Such hops are bulky and perishable, so frequently now hops are ground, pressed into small pellets, and hermetically sealed. A more controversial practice is the extraction of the active chemicals as an oil. Many people consider that the flavour imparted by hop oil is inferior to that of full or pelletised hops. Only leaf or pelletised hops may be used in the copper to satisfy CAMRA's definition of pure beer. Some popular hop types are: Fuggles and Goldings, old-fashioned English varieties; Wye Challenger and Northdown, high-alpha strains bred at Wye agricultural college; and Target, a powerful hop which is

also resistant to the fungus disease, wilt, which attacks English hop fields.

hop (to) *(brewing)* to add hops to the wort or the fermenting beer.

hop aphid a pest which attacks 95% of world hop production.

hop back *(brewing)* a large flat sieving vessel with a perforated false bottom which filters out the spent hops after boiling together with any coagulated protein. Modern hop backs, where leaf hops are no longer used, often separate the residues by centrifugal action. See whirlpools.

Hop Back Brewery PLC. Salisbury brewery famous for its bottled beers and colourful labels.

hop bag *(homebrewing)* a nylon bag used in home-brewing to contain the hops during the boil as an alternative to a false bottom or hop back.

hop bine the hop plant.

hop bitterness coefficient *(brewing)* the coefficient obtained by multiplying the percentage of alpha acid in the hops by the number of ounces of hops to be boiled.

hop broker a purveyor of hops.

hop cone the hop flower head, rich in aromatic resins, oils, tannin and acids. Also referred to as the blossom or flower.

hop essential oils hop oils – chemical extract of the active components of the hop flower.

hop extract *(homebrewing)* essential substances obtained from hops and used in homebrew kits.

hop field where hops are grown and harvested.

hop flour former name for lupulin, the fine, yellow powder which contains the essential oils and bitter resins.

hop garden the Kentish name for a hop field.

hop kiln the hop drying house, more often known as an oast house.

hop oil a chemical extract of the active components of the hop flower. See hop.

hop pellet pulverised and pressed hop flowers, which can be approx. 30% more bitter by weight than when used loose. Only pelletised or leaf hops may be used in the copper to satisfy CAMRA's definition of pure beer. See hop.

hop pillow a pillow stuffed with fresh hops to help induce sleep as some of the aromatic oils in the hop flowers have narcotic effects.

hop plugs loose hops which have been compressed into a bung under pressure.

hop pocket a very large sack containing fresh hops. See hop.

hop separator *(brewing)* a hop back.

hop shoots the first growth of the germinating seed of the hop plant. Harvested and eaten as a delicacy, particularly in Belgium.

hop utilisation *(brewing)* a measurement of the theoretical bittering efficiency against the actual.

hop yard the Southwest Midlands name for a hop field, where hops are grown.

hopped wort the wort in the copper, which has been boiled vigorously with the hops.

hopper a machine for harvesting hops.

hoppiness *(beer evaluation)* pertaining to the volatile oils of the hop plant.

hoppy *(beer evaluation)* having a hop aroma, taste and aftertaste.

hordeum distichon two-row barley.

hordeum vulgare six-row barley.

horsing a brick, wooden or metal framework on which the casks are set up in the cellar. Also known as thralls or stillage.

Horticultural Research International a science department at Wye College, Kent, funded by the Ministry of Agriculture, which researches hop disease and pest attack, and develops new hop varieties which are resistant to these problems. Abbreviation: HRI.

Hoskins & Oldfield Brewery set up by two members of Leicester's famous brewing family, Philip and Stephen Hoskins, in 1984, after the sale of the old Hoskins brewery.

hospoda *(Czech)* pub.

host term used by the trade press to refer to licensees and their spouses.

hostelry originally a public house offering accommodation; synonymous with an inn. Now used somewhat pretentiously for any pub.

hostinec *(Czech)* pub.

hot break *(brewing)* the flocculation of protein in the wort during boiling.

hot liquor *(brewing)* hot water.

houblon *(French)* hop.

House brand a trade name identifying a particular beer as having been brewed by, or exclusively for, the pub. CAMRA deplores the practise of pubs advertising beers as "house brands" when the beers are not produced by, or exclusively for, the pub.

House of Horrors early 1980s pub phenomenon popularised by Whitbread. Take a stuffed gorilla, a wickerwork frog, half a tailor's dummy, a tractor wheel, and pray that the customers put up with it for more than two weeks!

Houston Brewing Company family-owned brewery attached to the Fox and Hounds pub.

Hoxton Heavy a cask-conditioned organic beer, brewed by Pitfield (London).

HRI *(abbreviation)* Horticultural Research International: a science department at Wye College, Kent, funded by the Ministry of Agriculture, which researches hop disease and pest attack, and develops new hop varieties which are resistant to these problems.

Huddersfield Brewing Company brewery launched in 1997 in Huddersfield.

Hue a traditional Vietnamese lager.

hugget Scottish term for a Hogshead: a 54-gallon cask.

Hull Brewery Company Limited latest version formed in 1994: the name has been attached to various enterprises.

humle *(Danish)* hops.

Humpty Dumpty Brewery opened in 1998 in Norfolk.

humulone a soft resin, present in the hop flower. Also called alpha resin.

humulus lupulus botanical name for the hop plant.

Huntsman Ales the popular name for Eldridge Pope's beers and pubs in Dorset. The huntsman figure is also used by Tetleys in the north; both breweries adopted the design for use in their areas in the 1920s, but in 1935 Eldridge Pope. redesigned the jovial character with the monocle to avoid confusion.

Hurlimann Switzerland's best-known brewery, based in Zurich, which brews a very strong beer, Samichlaus (Santa Claus), containing a mighty 14 per cent alcohol.

hvede *(Danish)* wheat.

Hydes' Brewery Ltd. M a n c h e s t e r brewing company first established at the Crown Brewery Audenshaw in 1863.

hydrolysis *(brewing)* a chemical reaction in which a compound reacts with the OH ion resulting in the production of other compounds.

hydrometer *(brewing)* equipment used to measure the specific gravity of wort during fermentation.

IBU *(abbreviation)* International Bittering Units: a standard system of units for measuring the bitterness content of beer based on parts per million content of alpha acids.

Iceni Brewery started in 1995 and from mid-1998 the beer range has been produced in bottle-conditioned form.

imbottigliata dalla *(Italian)* bottled by.

Ind Coope a name from the past and one of the earliest national brewers, with breweries in Romford and Burton, which in 1961 merged with Ansells and Tetley Walker to form Allied Breweries. Marston's keeps the name alive with its Ind Coope Burton Ale.

independent brewer a family or privately owned brewery, not part of a conglomerate. In the UK these are traditional 'family brewers' and micro-breweries. There are currently (2001) 400 independent brewers in the UK.

India Pale Ale name originally applied to strong pale ales of high keeping qualities and remarkable yeast stability, brewed to mature and come into condition (in cask) on the long sea voyage to India. Tradition has it that the fame of Bass as a brewer rests on the accidental shipwreck of a consignment of Bass's Pale Ale bound from Liverpool to India; the casks were retrieved and drunk eagerly, creating immediate home demand for more. The term is now debased by being applied to draught bitters of relatively ordinary qualities, often designated simply by the initials IPA.

infection *(brewing)* the growth of any microorganism in wort or beer which is detrimental to the flavour of the beer.

infusion *(brewing)* the British method of mashing, i.e. extracting the fermentable material from the grist simply by leaving it to soak in the hot liquor for several hours. See also decoction.

initial heat *(brewing)* the temperature at which mashing is started.

inn traditionally a licensed hostelry catering for travellers.

inn sign a signboard outside a pub giving, often pictorially, the name of the pub and details of the brewery which owns it. Some pictorial signs, such as those of Palmer's of Bridport, are works of art, and the 'collecting' of inn signs is a hobby in itself which can often reveal much of the social, industrial, or feudal history of a locality.

Institute of Brewing professional body for the commercial brewer.

insufficient attenuation *(brewing)* occurs when the final gravity is higher than it should be.

Interbrew an international brewery group, resulting from a merger in Belgium between Stella Artois and Piedboeuf.

International Bittering Units international standard method of assessing bitterness in beers. Abbreviation: IBU.

in tonnen gerijpt *(Flemish)* cask-conditioned.

Inveralmond Brewery Ltd. established in 1997 to become the first brewery in Perth for more than 30 years.

inversion *(brewing)* the breakdown of sucrose into glucose and fructose.

invert sugar *(brewing)* a form of easily fermentable sugar (fructose and glucose) used in brewing as an adjunct or for priming.

IPA India Pale Ale. The name originally applied to strong pale ales of high keeping qualities and remarkable yeast stability, brewed to mature and come into condition (in cask) on the long sea voyage to India. Tradition has it that the fame of Bass as a brewer rests on the accidental shipwreck of a consignment of Bass's Pale Ale bound from Liverpool to India; the casks were retrieved and drunk eagerly, creating immediate home demand for more. The term is now debased by being applied to draught bitters of relatively ordinary qualities.

Iris Rose Brewery opened in 1997 just to brew for its own three hotels but now supplying other outlets.

Irish Brewing Company craft brewer in Co. Kildare, Eire, producing a pilsner to the 1516 German Purity Standard.

Irish moss *(brewing)* a marine algae sometimes added to aid protein coagulation during the final stages of boiling, which clears the wort. Also called Carragheen.

isinglass *(brewing)* another name for finings: a clearing agent made from the swim bladder of the sturgeon fish.

Isle of Skye Brewing Company established in 1995 and growing.

iso-alpha-acids bittering compounds formed during the boiling of alpha acids. Also called iso-humulones.

iso-alpha-acid hop extract *(brewing)* isomerised hop extract.

iso-humulones *(brewing)* bittering compounds formed when alpha acids are boiled. Also called iso-alpha-acids.

isoamyl acetate banana ester.

isomerisation *(brewing)* the extraction of hop bitterness. The alpha and beta acids are isomerised (a chemical optical inversion of the molecule) during boiling. This results in more solubility and higher bitterness levels.

isomerised hop extract   *(brewing)*
   iso-alpha-acid hop extract.

Itchen Valley Brewery Limited
   Hampshire brewery founded in
   1997.

Jacob's ladder a conveyor for transporting casks of ale from the cellar to the pub or brewery.

James Squire convicted highway robber and publican, who reputedly produced the first commercial ale in the new colony of Australia, at Kissing Point on the banks of the Parramatta River, west of Sydney. The actual date is unknown, but it was probably some time late in 1795, at his tavern The Malting Shovel.

Japanese rice beer sake.

JC & RH Palmer Ltd. Palmers' Old Brewery in West Dorset is Britain's only thatched brewery.

jednactka *(Czech)* a beer of 11 degree strength.

Jenlain a town in northern France, home to the Brasserie Duyck.

Jenlain a classic Bière de Garde (laying-down beer) of northern France, from the town of Jenlain near Valenciennes. Top-fermented and unpasteurised, it has an alcohol content of 6.5 per cent.

Jennings Bros PLC brewing since 1874 at the Castle Brewery, Cockermouth, Cumbria. Founded in 1828.

jets d'houblon *(French)* hop shoots.

jetting machine a bottle-washing machine.

Jever a German Pilsener.

John O'Gaunt Brewing Co. Ltd. shares the equipment of the Parish Brewery.

John Smith's John Smith is the northern arm of Scottish Courage, taken over in 1970, and arch Tadcaster rival of the independent and once related Samuel Smith. The magnificent Victorian brewery, built in 1884, did not brew any real ale at all for ten years, until cask John Smith's Bitter was reintroduced in 1984.

Jong *(Flemish)* a young lambic.

Joseph Holt Group PLC Manchester family brewery established in 1849. See Holt.

Judges Real Ale Brewery Ltd. set up in 1992 in Birmingham.

jug a vessel for holding and pouring liquids, often pear-shaped with a handle and a lip.

jug *(slang)* a glass of beer.

Jug and Bottle the off-sales part of a pub, usually served via a hatch from the main bar, traditionally where draught beer was served in jugs or bottled beer was bought to be taken home.

juke box originating in US bars, a machine for playing music of a customer's choice on payment of a sum of money.

Julebrygg *(Norwegian)* Christmas beer brewed since 1993; lighter than Juleøl (max. 4.75% ABV).

Juleøl   *(Norwegian)*   traditional Christmas beer, dark brown/red in colour with a sweetish aftertaste (max. 7.0% ABV).

juniper   a shrub with berry-like cones which can be used to flavour beer.

Jupiler   a Dutch lager.

Juwards Brewery Somerset concern founded in 1994.

JW Lees & Co (Brewers) Ltd.   a family-owned Manchester brewery founded in 1828.

Kaiserdom a Bavarian brewery in Bamberg which specialises in the town's famous Rauchbier.

kamertemperatur *(Dutch)* room temperature.

keeve Scottish term for a bulk barrel (36 gallons).

keg short for 'keg beer'. Keg beer is pressurised brewery- conditioned or processed beer, usually pasteurised. Keg beer was first developed by Watneys in the 1930s for export and sale in clubs or hotels which could not handle cask. Flowers first promoted it in the 1950s, and then it really took off in the 1960s with the arrival of the national brewers and their need for an easy-to-handle product which could be sold all over the country – at a premium price, naturally!

keg a container for brewery-conditioned beer.

keg (to) to draw beer from the fermenting vessels to the kegs.

Keg Buster *(Campaign)* cartoon character created by artist Bill Tidy, who epitomises the fighting spirit of the British beer drinker, as seen with the rise of CAMRA, the Campaign for Real Ale.

Kelham Island Brewery Ltd. South Yorkshire brewery formed in 1990 in the back yard of the Fat Cat pub.

Keltek Brewery Cornish company that started brewing again in 1999.

Kemptown Brewery Co. established in 1989 and built in the tower tradition behind the Hand in Hand, in Brighton.

Kent Garden Brewery Faversham based brewery.

Kent Goldings an English hop variety with an alpha acid content of approximately 5%.

kettle *(brewing)* another name for the copper, the brewery vessel in which the wort and the hops are boiled.

kettle hops copper hops.

keystone a wooden or nylon bung put into the tap hole of a cask. The centre of a keystone is partially bored through by the spigot, and the tap is driven in through this piece, leaving the outer wooden ring as a 'washer' sealing the tap into the cask.

kieselguhr *(brewing)* a mineral powder used in some breweries as a filter medium substance for clarification or fining.

kieselguhr filter *(brewing)* a filter which consists of a layer of kieselguhr through which the beer is pumped. Particles are trapped by the kieselguhr bed.

kil see kilderkin.

kild see kilderkin.

kilderkin an 18-gallon (or two firkin) cask, known as a 'kil' or 'kild'.

kiln *(malting)* a large drying chamber heated with hot air. The hot air is released through the perforations in the floor to dry the malt. Kilning stops further modification and induces malt flavours.

kiln-dried hops freshly picked hops which have been dried in a hop kiln (oust house) to retain their soft resins and essential oils.

kiln fan a rotating device to generate a current of air within a kiln.

kiln floor *(malting)* any of the platforms within a kiln.

kilning *(malting)* the final stage in the malting process: Malt is placed into kilns at high temperatures in order to halt modification. Also known as curing.

Kindl one of West Berlin's two major breweries, famous for its white beer. See Berliner Weisse.

King & Barnes traditional Sussex family brewery in Horsham, that closed for business in 2000.

King & Smart Lincolnshire Brewery, working since mid-1999.

Kings Head Brewing Co. Ipswich brewery.

Kirin the giant of Japanese brewing, best known for its lager (4.5 per cent alcohol). Also produces a rarer stout.

Kitchen Brewery Ltd. Huddersfield based.

klar *(German:"clear")* filtered.

kloeckera apiculata a lambic yeast strain.

Kloster *(German: "monastery")* an Abbey beer.

Kneipe *(German)* pub or night bar.

Kölsch Cologne's own top-fermented German beer style, of medium strength (3.7% alcohol) soft taste, and pale colour. Only a few breweries in Cologne are allowed to use the name. The best-known is Kuppers. Kölsch glasses are easily recognisable – they are tall and slender.

kräusen (to) *(brewing)* to add a small quantity of partially fermented wort to a beer to induce further fermentation.

kräusening *(brewing)* the German equivalent of gyling, by which a portion of vigorously fermenting wort from primary fermentation is added to 'green' beer to induce natural conditioning. Also used as an alternative to priming with sugars.

Kriek *(Flemish: "black cherry")* a Belgian Gueuze beer in which the second fermentation has been caused by adding black cherries or cherry juice.

Kristallweizen *(German:"crystal wheat")* clear, filtered wheat beer.

kro *(Danish)* pub.

Kronen   the oldest Dortmund brewery and the most popular in the German city itself producing the fine Dortmunder, Kronen Export (5.2 per cent alcohol), and the weaker, award-winning Classic.

kruiden   *(Dutch; Flemish)*   herbs; spices.

kruidenbier   Flemish ale spiced with herbs, particularly coriander.

Kulminator   a strong German Eisbock – full name Kulminator 28 Urtyp Hell – is lagered for nine months by the Bavarian EKU (Erste Kulmbacher) brewery near Bayreuth, and frozen to increase its strength by the removal of water ice, giving it an alcohol content of 12.4 per cent.

Kuppers   the most widely exported brand of Kölsch (4.5 per cent alcohol), the unique light ale of Cologne, Germany (German: Köln).

kvasnicove pivo   *(Czech)*   unfiltered beer.

kvass   traditional russian beer from water, rye flour or rye bread, malt, yeast, sugar, peppermint leaves and sultanas. Sold by street vendors.

La Gazette des Eswards *(French)* a quarterly journal produced by the French organisation Les Amis de la Bière, which promotes the beer culture in France.

La Trappe a Dutch Trappist ale (6.5 per cent alcohol), from the Schaapskooi abbey brewery.

Labatt Brewing Company Canadian brewery founded in 1847 by John Kinder Labatt. Based in Ontario and part of Belgium-based Interbrew.

label a piece of paper which is glued to the beer bottle and which gives the name and other information relating to the beer. CAMRA supports legislation to bring beer into line with other foodstuffs, specifically regarding ingredient listing and per cent alcohol by volume.

labologist a collector of beer bottle labels. A labologists' society started in 1959 after a Guinness promotion encouraged the hobby.

lace see lacing.

lacing the residues of the head adhering to the side of the glass.

lactic acid a tart acid found in infected beer.

lactobacillus delbrueckii a strain of yeast combining a top-fermenting yeast and a lactobacillus bacterium, used in Berliner Weisse.

lactobacillus infection *(brewing)* see microbial infection.

lactobacillus inoculation *(brewing)* the deliberate introduction of a lactic acid bacterium. Used for commercially produced African native sorghum beer. Also a component of Lambic beers.

lage gisting *(Dutch)* bottom-fermented.

lager beer fermented with the 'bottom-fermentation' yeast Saccharomyces uvarum (formerly S. carlsbergensis). Production of lager differs from ale in several other respects: lower modified malts are used in the decoction rather than the infusion mash system; the liquor is generally soft and low in mineral salts; continental, seedless, low alpha acid hops are used (e.g. Saaz or Hallertau); primary fermentation is at a lower temperature than for ale, and secondary fermentation in closed conditioning tanks takes place at around 0°C for a lengthy period, often exceeding four weeks. Few British-brewed lagers conform to European practices, despite their European names. They are of lower gravity than their European equivalents. European lagers are often not pasteurised or filtered, but merely racked bright off the dormant yeast at the end of fermentation, and are then dispensed from the cask under the pressure generated by their natural conditioning. British lagers are normally filtered, pasteurised, re-carbonated, and dispensed under CO_2 pressure from kegs via flash coolers. Some smaller UK breweries are beginning to brew 'real lager'.

lager malt malted barley which is kilned at a low temperature to provide a very pale colour (3EBC).

lager øl *(Danish)* lager-style beer.

lager yeast 'bottom-fermenting' yeast. Lager yeast works at a cooler temperature than ale yeast and sinks to the bottom of the fermenting vessel.

lagering the storing of lager beers in near-freezing storage rooms or cellars for several weeks, sometimes months. (German: lagern = to store)

lahvove pivo *(Czech)* bottled beer.

lambic the unique 'wild' beers of Belgium produced by spontaneous fermentation. Wild yeasts from the air ferment these wheat brews from the Senne Valley, west of Brussels, giving them a unique sour taste and an alcohol content of 4.5 per cent. Lambic beers must, by law, contain a minimum of 30 per cent unmalted wheat in the mash, which must contain at least five per cent grain. Lambic is usually blended to form Gueuze, and other variations are Faro (sweetened), Kriek (cherry), and Framboise (raspberry).

Lambic Doux clear, filtered, sweetened Lambic.

Langton Brewery Leicestershire based brewery.

lapin à la bière *(French; culinary)* rabbit with beer.

Larkins Brewery Ltd. founded in 1986, based on the Royal Tunbridge Wells Brewery.

last orders the words used by the landlord or landlady to remind customers to purchase their last beers of the evening, allowing 'drinking-up time' before 'closing time'.

Late Cluster an American variety of general purpose hop.

late hopping the addition of a quantity of aroma hops to the brew kettle during the last 15 or 20 minutes of the boil in order to restore flavour and aroma.

late hops aroma hops, low in alpha acid, which are added to the brew kettle towards the end of the boil. They do not impart much bitterness to the brew. Also added as dry hops to the cask after filling. To satisfy CAMRA's definition of a pure beer, only cone or compressed hops may be used as post-fermentation bittering substances.

lates *(slang)* term for drinks sold after permitted hours of opening.

lauter (to) *(brewing)* to empty the mash tun or other vessel. Also known as 'to run off'. (German: läutern = to clean).

lauter tun *(brewing)* a vessel which holds the mash and separates wort from spent grain. Now common in big commercial breweries and all lager breweries. These systems use a mash mixing vessel, a mash cooking vessel (mash copper or cereal cooker), a lauter tun or mash separator, and a wort copper; can also be used for infusion mashing. Lauter tuns incorporate rotating knives or blades to keep the bottom of the mash open and give a fast run-off of wort.

Leadmill Brewery Co. Nottingham brewery established in February 1999.

Leatherbritches Brewery housed behind the Bentley Brook Inn in Ashbourne, Derbyshire.

lees the sediment at the bottom of the bottle or cask comprising mainly dead yeast, bits of hop and proteins.

Lees one of Manchester's surviving independent family breweries. It was founded in 1828. All its pubs serve real ale.

Leffe a Belgian 'abbey beer'.

legless *(slang)* description of someone who is drunk.

length *(brewing)* the quantity of wort brewed in each brewing operation.

Leopard the smallest of New Zealand's three brewing groups. Jointly owned by Heineken and Malayan Breweries.

Les Amis de la Bière *(French: "friends of beer")* French organisation formed in 1986 to promote the beer culture in France; affiliated to the European Beer Consumers' Union. It produces a quarterly journal "La Gazette des Eswards".

Letece a French dark lager.

Lettøl *(Norwegian)* light beer (max. 2.5% ABV).

Lev *(Czech: "lion")* a range of beers from the Czech Republic: Lion Lager; Lion Double Bock; Black Lion.

levain *(French)* yeast.

levure *(French)* yeast.

Leyden Brewery Bury brewery constructed by Brian Farnworth in 1999.

Lezak *(Czech)* a beer with a strength of 11° or higher.

Liberty an American aroma hop variety with an alpha acid content of 3.5-4%. Used for German-style lagers.

licence 'under licence': when one brewery grants another, often abroad, permission to brew its recipe. Usually this results in an inferior product.

license (to) to grant or give a licence for the sale of alcohol. CAMRA believes that licensing justices should have to give reasons in writing for all their decisions.

licensing hours the times during which a pub is legally permitted to sell alcohol. In August 1988 the government introduced all-day weekday opening in pubs. This followed a long campaign by CAMRA. Scottish all-day opening showed the way. In 1995 Sunday afternoon opening was introduced. As of June 2001, there is still no planned legislation to introduce 24-hour pub opening.

licensing justices a body of up to 15 ordinary lay magistrates who sit on local licensing committees and deal with licence applications and renewals. CAMRA believes that licensing law should be formulated on the basis of a comprehensive national strategy, which is aimed at avoiding the excessive consumption of alcohol by individuals, and at minimising the socially unacceptable consequences of over-indulgence.

Lichfield Brewery began brewing in 1992. Based in Derbyshire.

Lidstones Brewery Suffolk based and active since 1998.

Liefmans Belgian brewery based in Oudenaarde, a town famous for its top-fermenting brown ales.

Liefmans produce the best in huge litre bottles, notably Goudenband Speciaal Provisie.

Liefmans a cherry or raspberry lambic.

light ale a low-gravity (hence light in body, not necessarily light in colour) bottled ale, usually of less strength than 'ordinary' bitter, though of higher condition and lower hoppiness. A Scottish 'light' or 60/-ale is normally a dark-coloured draught beer of around 1030-1035 OG, not unlike an English mild.

light amber *(beer evaluation)* a colour definition.

light beer any American low-calorie beer, which does not contain dextrins or a low-calorie beer with an alcohol content ranging between 2.8 to 4% abv.

light straw *(beer evaluation)* a colour definition.

light struck *(beer evaluation)* having a distinctive smell, which Americans would recognise as that of a skunk, which results from the beer having been exposed to sunlight or fluorescent light. Also called sunstruck.

limit attenuation *(brewing)* an alternative term for final degree of attenuation.

Lindemans Belgian farmhouse brewery at Vlezenbeek producing wild lambic beers.

lined glasses *(Campaign)* half pint and pint glasses which have a line to indicate a half pint, full pint measure respectively. CAMRA campaigns for the mandatory use of lined glasses in all pubs to ensure that drinkers receive a full measure and believes that appropriate Weights & Measures legislation should exist which defines a pint of beer as 20fl oz of liquid excluding any head of froth or foam.

Linfit Brewery brew pub from 1800s that recommenced brewing in 1982.

lining the marking of beer glasses during manufacture, with a line to indicate a specific measure. The most important line for beer drinkers is the one that shows a full pint has been poured. CAMRA campaigns for the use of lined glasses to be mandatory.

lion a symbol: over the years many breweries have used, and continue to use, the lion as a symbol or name. Morrell's of Oxford used a lion trademark and Lion Nathan is one of the biggest brewing groups in the world. Even Löwenbrau means 'lions' brew'.

Lion Nathan massive multinational brewing beers in New Zealand, Australia and China. Known for its Castlemaine XXXX and Steinlager brands.

liquefaction *(brewing)* the enzymic process by which alpha-amylase degrades starch into soluble polysaccharides. Also known as gelatinisation.

liquid yeast yeast in suspension.

liquor *(brewing)* water. Also called mashing liquor; brewing liquor; brewing water.

liquorice Mediterranean shrub, the dried root of which can be used to add colour and flavour to dark beers.

liquorice *(beer evaluation)* having a sweet liquorice flavour often resulting from the use of dark malts and thus often a characteristic of dark beers and stouts.

litre metric unit of measurement equivalent to approximately 13/4 Imperial pints.

Little Creatures Brewery Australian concern using brewery shipped from Canada in 13 containers and now brewing LIVE, a bottle conditioned pale ale style beer.

lively a term applied to a bottled beer which froths upon opening.

Liverpool Brewing Company a brew pub.

Lizard Point a cask-conditioned organic beer brewed by the Organic Brewery.

Lloyds Country Beers Ltd. sells beers brewed at the John Thompson Inn in the Midlands.

local popular name for a neighbourhood pub with local trade, or the name for a pub regularly used by a person.

Local guide *(Campaign)* a list of real ale pubs surveyed and published by a regional branch of CAMRA.

Lokal *(German)* pub.

London Stout a name now chiefly used by breweries outside Britain, like Moosehead of Canada.

long pull a serving over the measure, as for example 'a generous half' into a pint glass. This is a specific offence under the Licensing Act, whereas serving short measure is not (it is dealt with under weights and measures legislation).

loose head a light froth of large irregular bubbles on the top of the beer after dispense, which rapidly collapse.

loose hops the hop cones, dried after picking.

Loss of amenity policies *(Campaign)* a campaigning initiative by CAMRA to persuade local authorities to include in their District Plans a presumption against loss of village amenities.

lounge a pub room which is more comfortably furnished than the public bar, and where drink prices, as a consequence, are higher.

Lovibund the scale used by American brewers to measure the wort and colour of beer. See SRM. Abbreviation: °L.

low alpha hops a new variety of disease and pest resistant hop, developed by HRI at Wye, that has good aroma properties but moderate bitterness. Not currently commercially available.

low trellis hops alternative name for dwarf hops.

Löwenbrau *(German: "lion's brew")* the world-famous 'Lion' brewery of Munich.

Lublin a Polish aroma hop with an alpha acid content of 2-4%.

lupulin the sticky yellow powder in the hop cone which contains the essential oils and soft resins, which give the hop its bittering and aromatic qualities.

lupulin glands tiny yellow sacs containing lupulin, found at the base of the petals of the hop cone.

lupulone alternative name for beta acid.

LVA *(abbreviation)* Licensed Victuallers' Association: a voluntary society of landlords devoted to preserving their interests and the interests of 'the trade'. LVAs are arranged roughly on licensing districts. Complementary to the LVA is the 'auxiliary', an association of publicans' wives primarily devoted to charitable and social activities.

lys øl *(Danish)* light beer.

maceration the softening of the barley by steeping.

Mackie a tall fount: a tall pillar-tap mounting stationed on a bar, used to dispense traditional beers in Scotland.

MacLachlans Brew Bar Glasgow city-centre bar with its own in-house brewery.

Maclay Scottish brewery in Alloa that stopped brewing in 1999. Forth Brewery supplies its pubs with cask beers.

Maes a Belgian brewery, well-known for its Pils, but also brews an Abbaye-style beer called Grimbergen.

magnesium sulphate Epsom salts, a mineral found in, or added to water for brewing to promote yeast activity. Formula: $MgSO_4 7H_2O$.

Maibock *(German: "May bock")* a pale bock beer brewed to be ready for drinking in the spring.

Maillard reactions *(brewing)* a series of chemical reactions which result in the production of melanoidins. Also called browning reactions.

maize syrup high glucose or high maltose syrups.

Mallard Brewery Nottingham mini brewery since 1994.

malt barley which has been partially germinated and then kilned to convert the starch into fermentable sugars, so that the majority of the carbohy-drate material that is fermented by yeast turns into alcohol. Malt also gives body and flavour to beer and adds to its colour. Malt is often known as 'the soul of beer'.

malt (to) to kiln dry partially germinated barley.

malt d'orge *(French)* barley malt.

malt extract syrup obtained by infusing malt. If the wort extracted from the mash is boiled under a very low pressure, or passed over thin film evaporators, most of the water content can be evaporated to leave a treacly syrup which contains the sugars extracted from the malt. Specialised companies produce malt extract, mostly for homebrew kits, but many brewers also use extract to supplement or modify their mash and some pub breweries avoid the expense of installing a mash tun by using only extract, made up with water, put directly into the copper.

malt extract brewing a convenient method of brewing for which a mash is not required – all of the ingredients are boiled vigorously for an hour and a half and then strained into the fermentation bin. Mainly used by homebrewers.

malt hopper a funnel-shaped reservoir from which the dried malt is channelled to the the mill for milling.

malt kiln *(malting)* a kiln in a maltings for drying and roasting partially germinated barley.

malt liquor an American beer style in which strong unhopped lagers are fermented out to produce a thin but potent drink. Popular in run-down inner city areas in the USA.

malt shovel *(malting)* a wooden shovel used to turn over germinating barley at floor maltings.

Malt Shovel Brewery Chuck Hahn, a well-known commercial brewer in Australia, built his own brewery. He renamed it in honour of Australia's first commercial brewer, and called his first beer James Squire Original Amber Ale.

malt store the top floor (below the roof, where the liquor tanks are housed) of a traditional brewery, where the grain is stored and weighed.

malt stout popular name for bottled stout.

malt sugar maltose: a sugar formed by the enzymic hydrolysis of starch.

malt syrup *(brewing)* a concentrated malt extract used in the mash to help convert grain or adjuncts, or in the copper (when it is called 'copper syrup') to extend brew length or adjust gravity.

malt tails beard.

malt tannins tannic acids in malt.

malt tax a Government tax levied until 1880, when beer duty was introduced.

malted barley barley which has been steeped in water and allowed to germinate, before being kilned.

maltiness *(beer evaluation)* pertaining to the malty aftertaste.

malting floor *(malting)* traditionally the vast flat area in a maltings where the barley is spread after steeping prior to germination.

maltings the buildings where raw barley is converted into malt by the maltster.

malto *(Italian)* malt.

maltodextrins the compounds of maltose and dextrins.

Malton Brewery Company founded in the stable block at the rear of the Crown Hotel in Wheelgate, Malton, North Yorkshire in 1984.

maltose a fermentable sugar formed by the enzymic hydrolysis of starch.

maltster a trained official responsible for overseeing the malting process in a maltings. Similar to the head brewer in a brewery. Leading maltsters which supply organic grain are: Crisps, Muntons, Simpsons and Warminster.

malty *(beer evaluation)* having a strong malt aroma and aftertaste; a characteristic of pale malts.

Malvern Hills Brewery Ltd.   opened in a former explosive store in a disused quarry.

Malz *(German)* malt.

Malzbier *(German: "malt beer")* a dark beer, with a high malt content and low (if any) alcohol content.

Man in the Moon Brewery   opened in 1996 in Lutterworth, Leicestershire.

mandatory rate relief *(Campaign)* a campaigning initiative by CAMRA to lobby for country pubs to share the same right to mandatory relief from business rates (at present up to 100%) enjoyed by shops and post offices in village locations.

Mansfield Brewery PLC

Nottinghamshire brewery founded in 1855. Part of Wolverhampton & Dudley Breweries.

Manx Pure Beer Act 1874 Act of Parliament to protect the purity of The Isle of Man beers. The Isle of Man decrees that its ales shall be brewed only from malt, hops, and sugar.

Marble Brewery working since 1998 in the Marble Arch Inn in North Manchester.

Marches Ales set up in 1995. Herefordshire based.

maris otter a strain of barley regarded as the best quality for ale malt and grown in England and Wales.

market extension an extension to normal permitted licensing hours made under an order of general exception that originally allowed certain pubs to open later on market days. Particularly common in the market towns of northern England.

Marston Moor Brewery set up in 1983 near York.

Marston, Thompson & Evershed PLC

Marston's from Burton upon Trent are a subsidiary of Wolverhampton & Dudley Breweries. The only brewery still using the Burton Union system of fermentation for Pedigree Bitter.

Märzen *(German: "March")* a full-bodied (5.5 per cent alcohol) bottom-fermented lager originating in Vienna but developed in Munich as their stronger Märzen brews which were fermented over the summer for drinking at the Oktoberfest. A special malt is used, which gives Märzen a mild, malty flavour. The classic Märzen is copper coloured.

mash *(brewing)* a mixture of mashed malt and heated water.

mash (to) *(brewing)* to infuse malt and water in the mash tun, to extract the fermentable materials from the malt. The malt is usually mixed with hot liquor in a mashing machine (Steeles masher) directly into the mash tun. In smaller operations the mash tun may be partially filled with hot water and the milled malt added to it to form a porridge-like mass. The mixture is left to steep. During the mash enzymes in the malt, activated by the hot water, convert the starches into sugars and these sugars pass into the liquid. After several hours the liquid, which is now the sweet wort, is run off, and the spent grains are emptied to be sold off as cattle food. See also decoction and infusion.

Mash and Air Manchester brew-restaurant founded in 1997 in a converted mill. Spawned a London version and then was forced to close.

mash copper *(brewing)* see mash kettle.

mash filter *(brewing)* a filter press fitted with plates for filtering the mash.

mash kettle *(brewing)* a metal vat used in decoction mashing for boiling part of the mash. Also called mash copper.

mash tun *(brewing)* the vessel in which the mash is infused. The mash tun has a squat cylindrical shape, surrounded by considerable insulation to allow the mash temperature to be maintained. The vessel has a false floor of perforated plates which retain the grains as the wort is run off.

mashing in *(brewing)* the mixing of ground malt with water.

mashing liquor *(brewing)* water, natural or treated with calcium and magnesium sulphate, for mashing and brewing. Also called liquor; brewing liquor; brewing water.

mashing time *(brewing)* the required duration of the infusion or decoction mashing.

master brewer *(brewing)* a qualified brewer with a degree or diploma, who supervises the various brewing stages in a commercial brewery.

maturation the storage of beer for a period during which its quality improves as it matures and as impurities settle out.

Mauldons Brewery Sudbury company revived in 1982 by former Watneys' brewer Peter Mauldon.

Maypole Brewery established in 1995, brewing for local outlets.

McGlashan a tall fount: a tall pillar-tap mounting stationed on a bar, used to dispense traditional beers in Scotland.

McMullen & Sons Ltd. Hertfordshire's oldest independent brewery, founded in 1827.

mealie beer a beer brewed in southern Africa from millet or maize.

Meantime Brewing Co. Greenwich-based brewery run by Alistair Hook, formerly of Freedom and Mash.

media   *(Italian)* standard 'medium' glass of beer.

medicinal *(beer evaluation)* phenolic.

medium   Irish term for a half-pint of draught Guinness.

megakeggery derogatory term for the huge processed-beer factories built by the national brewers.

Meister   the Pils brand from Germany's largest brewery, Dortmunder Actien.

melanoidin a dark pigment formed in a Maillard reaction.

Melbourn Stamford brewery dating from 1825 that has recently closed and reopened a couple of times. Now owned by Samuel Smith of Tadcaster.

merger   when two or more companies combine. CAMRA believes that any merger should have to demonstrate clear benefit to the consumer before being allowed to proceed.

met gist   *(Dutch)* with yeast sediment.

metallic   *(beer evaluation)* having a metal aftertaste, sometimes caused when iron or corrosive metals are in contact with the beer.

metered dispense   a method of delivering beer from a cask to the counter dispenser using a metered positive displacement electric pump. The pump has a calibrated half-pint container from which the beer is displaced whenever a push-button at the dispense point is pressed.

méthode champinoise beers Belgian beers which have undergone a second or third fermentation in the bottle.

microbial infection   *(brewing)* contamination of the product by bacteria, wild yeasts etc.

microbrewery small-scale brewing operation. Equipment has been specially developed for brew pubs and small independent breweries.

Mighty Oak Brewing Company Ltd. established in 1996. Growing Essex brewery.

mild   an ale of low gravity and hop rate, hence rounder, usually slightly sweeter, and distinctly less bitter on the palate and in aroma than more highly hopped bitters. Mild is usually (but not always) darker in colour than bitter, through use of a higher-roast malt or caramel. There are considerable variations in mild styles.

mild ale malt malt, from high nitrogen barley. Colour 7 EBC.

Mild Day *(Campaign)* the first Saturday in May, where attention is focused on promoting this style of beer.

Mild Month *(Campaign)* a month's worth of campaigning to promote mild ale.

milk stout once a popular name for sweet stouts until leaned on by stricter product description laws.

Milk Street Brewery Frome brewery recently established.

mill (to) *(brewing)* to gently split the grain before mashing, to release the starch contained within the husks.

Miller American beer giant, second only to Anheuser-Busch, from the US brewing capital of Milwaukee, Wisconsin. Once famous for its 'High Life' lager, Miller is now known for popularising light beers.

Millers Thumb Brewing Co. American-style brew restaurant.

milling *(brewing)* the act of gently splitting the grain before mashing, to release the starch contained within the husks.

Milton Brewery supplying free trade outlets in the Cambridge area.

minging *(slang)* description of someone who is drunk.

mise en bouteille par *(French)* bottled by.

mit Hefe *(German: "with yeast")* unfiltered.

mix stout mixed half and half with bitter or mild. Also called Black and Tan.

modification *(malting)* the germination stage of the malting process (after steeping), when the barley starts to sprout shoots and the production of starch-modifying enzymes begins.

modified *(malting)* term used to describe the state of the malt after modification.

Molson the largest of Canada's 'Big Three' breweries, based in Quebec, producing a hoppier range of beers than Carling or Labatt.

monitor a piece of equipment which warns, checks, controls and/or keeps records of something or a process.

Moor Beer Company small brewery set up in 1996 on a former dairy farm in Somerset.

Moor's head a hop strainer comprising a perforated cone.

Moorhouses established 1863 and recently a growing brewery based in Burnley.

Moosehead Canadian brewery, which has become a cult in the United States, where its name and frontier setting in Nova Scotia and New Brunswick boost the appeal of its bolder range of beers.

Moravia a dry, hoppy bottled Pils (4.9 per cent alcohol) from the Holsten group of North Germany, brewed in Lüneburg.

Mordue Brewery won the Champion Beer of Britain award in 1997 with Workie Ticket.

mørk øl   *(Danish)* dark beer.

Morland   formerly Britain's second oldest independent brewery, dating back to 1711. The brewery was purchased and closed by Greene King in 2000, despite a vigorous campaign by CAMRA and Oxford residents.

Morning Advertiser   a daily newspaper for publicans.

Mort Subite   a lambic beer. This extravagantly named 'sudden death' is actually no stronger than other Belgian lambic beers. Also the name of a beer café in central Brussels.

Mother-in-Law   a mix of stout and bitter in equal quantities.

mouldy   *(beer evaluation)* having an earthy aftertaste, sometimes caused by unclean conditions for fermentation or damp, mouldy dispense conditions.

Moulin Hotel & Brewery   supplying local outlets since 1995.

Mount Hood an American aroma hop variety with an alpha acid content of 5-5.5%. Used for German-style lagers.

Mount Murray Brewing Co Ltd.   Isle of Man brewery set up in 1986 as a brew pub but in new premises since 1990.

Mousel & Clausen a Luxembourg lager.

mout *(Dutch)* malt.

mouth   the opening of a bottle.

mouthfeel *(beer evaluation)* a term applying to the sensation of body or viscosity in the mouth, created by dextrins and proteins in the beer.

mug popular name given to a half pint or full pint beer glass with a handle.

mull (to)   to heat ale gently with sugar and spices.

Mumme   a German Malzbier.

Münchener   the dark, malty, bottom-fermenting beers originating in Munich, which are now more often found in their pale ('hell') form. Has fairly low strength for German beer (around 4 per cent alcohol). In Munich a Münchener is drunk out of litre or possibly half litre glasses.

Munich Helles see Münchener.

Munich malt a darkish malt, traditionally used in the brewing of Munich beers. EBC: 12-30 .

Murphy   Irish stout brewers of Cork.

NABLABS *(abbreviation)* no alcohol or low alcohol beers.

nagisting in de fles
(Dutch/Flemish) bottle-fermented.

Nags Head Inn Pembrokeshire pub-brewery producing on an occasional basis.

NALHM *(abbreviation)* National Association of Licensed House Managers. The pub and club managers' trade union.

Nathan method a commercial process by which carbon dioxide is pumped into the beer to guarantee bright beer.

National Association of Licensed House Managers the pub and club managers' trade union. Abbreviation: NALHM.

National Guide *(Campaign)* a guide to real ale pubs which have been surveyed for quality by CAMRA members. Various guides are published by CAMRA.

National Hop Association of England formed in 1987 to look after the interests of English hop growers. Funds research programmes at Wye College in Kent. Abbreviation: NHA.

National Inventory of Historic Pub Interiors *(Campaign)* a campaigning initiative by CAMRA to extend the protection of statutory listing to unspoilt pub interiors, to ensure that the country's most interesting old pubs remain in use as pubs.

National Mild Day *(Campaign)* the first Saturday in May each year kicks off mild month, a month dedicated to the 'mild' style of beer.

National Union of Licensed Victuallers the pub tenants' national organisation, acting as an umbrella for local Licensed Victuallers' Associations (LVA). Abbreviation: NULV.

National Winter Ales Festival *(Campaign)* major festival held in January each year to celebrate particular beers brewed in the winter season.

natural condition the amount of dissolved carbon dioxide present in beer as a result of primary and secondary fermentation only.

naturally-conditioned a description of beer which still contains live yeast cells and continues to mature in the cask or bottle.

naturtrüb *(German:"naturally cloudy")* unfiltered.

near beer alcohol-free lager. Switzerland can lay claim to having created this beer style.

neck the narrower part of a bottle, just below the mouth.

Nelson Sauvin a new hop variety, developed in New Zealand, which imparts a fruity, grassy aroma, similar to that of Sauvignon Blanc wine.

Nephelometer *(brewing)* a device, calibrated in Formazin Haze Units or degrees Nephelos (° N) for measuring the haze in liquids.

Nethergate Brewery Co. small Suffolk brewer, set up in 1986.

nettle plant with stinging hairs, used prior to the hop to flavour beers.

Newby Wyke Brewery Grantham micro-brewery since 1998.

Newman the first American 'new wave' brewery to introduce a naturally-conditioned draught beer, Newman's Pale Ale, in the USA. Set up in Albany, New York, in 1981.

Newton & Ridley Coronation Street's famous brewers, who sadly don't exist beyond the TV set of the Rover's Return.

NHA *(abbreviation)* National Hop Association.

90/-Ales Scottish term for strong ales. See shilling.

nip a third of a pint; a common size for bottles of barley wine or very strong ale.

nipperkin an old name for a small measure of drink, usually less than half a pint.

nisseøl *(Danish)* dark, sweet winter/Christmas beer.

nitrates a salt in brewing liquor, which, if more than a trace is present, will affect fermentation.

nitrogen a colourless, odourless gas that is an essential constituent of proteins.

nitrogen content the amount of nitrogen in barley or malt given as a percentage of its weight.

Nitrokeg keg beer which is dispensed with a mix of carbon dioxide and nitrogen. CAMRA affirms that nitrokeg is just another form of brewery conditioned/keg beer and condemns the excessive hype surrounding such beers, which are not real ales.

noggin a unit of liquid measure equivalent to 1/4 pint, although often used to mean a small quantity.

non-alcoholic beer any malt drink which does not contain any per cent alcohol by volume.

non filtrée *(French)* unfiltered.

non pasteurisée *(French)* unpasteurised.

NORØL *(Norwegian)* Norske Ølvenners Landsforbund: a beer-drinkers consumer organisation founded in 1993, with similar aims to CAMRA.

North Cotswold Brewery
Warwickshire micro-brewery began in 1999 by brothers David and Roger Tilbrook.

North Country Hull Brewery, which was acquired by Northern Foods in 1972 and renamed North Country Breweries. In 1985 it was taken over by Mansfield Brewery. It sold mainly bright beers under the misleading Old Tradition name, but in 1982 did introduce a cask beer.

North Yorkshire Brewing Company
founded in 1989. Moved to Pinchinthorpe Hall, a medieval ancient monument that has its own spring water.

Northdown a British general purpose hop with an alpha acid content of 8.5-9.5%.

Northern Brewer a hop variety with an alpha acid content of 9-10%, suitable for brewing dark beers. Originated in Britain, but also grown in Southern Germany, Belgium and America.

Northumberland Brewery Ltd.
working since 1996 and now a solar-powered brewery on the Earth Balance community site.

nose *(beer evaluation)* the aroma of a beer.

not fully attenuated *(beer evaluation)* description of a sweet aftertaste, caused by the yeast not fully fermenting the sugars.

Nugget an American general purpose/bittering hop with an alpha acid content of 13-13.5%. Heavy, spicy aroma. Strong bittering.

NULV *(abbreviation)* National Union of Licensed Victuallers. The pub tenants' national organisation, acting as an umbrella for local LVAs (Licensed Victuallers' Association).

Nussdorf a Viennese Altbier.

nut brown popular name for bottled brown ales from breweries such as Adnams, Gales, and Shipstones.

nutty *(beer evaluation)* having a sherry-like aftertaste. Oxidation or a high storage temperature might be the causes.

Oakham Ales established in Rutland in 1993 and moved to former dole office in Peterborough in 1998. Under threat from commercial development.

Oakhill Brewery brewing in the Mendip Hills in Somerset since 1984 (formerly Beacon Brewery). The original brewery was founded in 1767 and burnt down in 1924.

Oakwell Brewery 1997 version of Barnsley brewery that closed in 1970 shortly after being taken over by John Smiths of Tadcaster.

oaky *(beer evaluation)* having an oak-wood aftertaste.

oast house popular name for a hop kiln, where hops are dried. Their distinctive cowled roofs make them a prominent feature of the Kent countryside.

oat malt adjunct used in oatmeal stout.

oats annual grass and its seeds. Flaked oats are used in some stout recipes.

oaty *(beer evaluation)* having a cereal aftertaste.

OB beers from Oldham Brewery of Manchester; the initials are usually printed on the side of a bell.

obergärig *(German)* top-fermented.

OBP *(Flemish; abbreviation)* Objectieve Bierproevers : "Objective beer tasters".

Objectieve Bierproevers *(Flemish)* "Objective beer tasters" – a Belgian beer consumer organisation founded in 1984. It differs from CAMRA in that it promotes the enjoyment of all beers rather than one particular style. Abbreviation: OBP.

Occasional Permissions a licence to sell alcohol (usually at an outside bar) for up to 24 hours, made to anyone over 18 years who is an accredited representative of a non-profit-making organisation. Four such licences may be granted each year (Occasional Permissions Act, 1983).

off-flavour *(beer evaluation)* having an impaired taste, either as a result of a contamination or poor brewing technique.

OG *(brewing; abbreviation)* original gravity: the British brewing industry's method of expressing the strength of beer. Pure water is defined as a gravity of 1000. Wort that is ready to start fermentation is denser than water, because of the fermentable material i.e. dissolved sugars. It is this density, the original gravity, which used to be measured to assess the excise duty. The higher the original gravity, the more fermentable material and thus a stronger finished beer. Most bitter beers have original gravities in the range 1035 to 1045, i.e. about 4% denser than water. Fermentation converts the sugars into alcohol, reducing the density of the liquid;

at the end of the fermentation period the beer reaches its final gravity. Final gravities are normally in the region 1008-1015. The higher the figure, the sweeter the beer. Compare: alcohol by volume (ABV). Often the original gravity and the alcohol by volume of a beer are the same. A lower original gravity is an indication of a well attenuated beer. A higher original gravity is an indication of residual sugars remaining in the beer.

O'Hanlon's Brewing Company Ltd.
Devon brewery set up in 1996.

ohne Hefe *(German: "without yeast")* filtered.

oils essential oils.

Okell & Son Ltd. Isle of Man brewery founded in 1874 by Dr Okell. The larger of the two independent breweries on the Isle of Man, brewing 'Falcon Ales' from its Douglas brewery.

Oktoberfest *(German: "October festival")* the great Munich beer festival held annually in October, where vast amounts of Märzenbier are traditionally drunk out of one-litre stoneware Steins in huge brewery 'tents'. A rival fair is held in Stuttgart.

øl *(Danish; Norwegian)* beer.

Old Ale now virtually synonymous with 'winter ale'. Most 'old ales' are produced and sold for a limited period in the year, usually between November and the end of February. Usually a rich, dark, high-gravity draught ale of considerable body. Such ales feature prominently at CAMRA's Winter Beer Festival.

Old Barn Brewery supplied its first brew to the Durham Beer Festival in 1998.

Old Bear Brewery founded in 1993 by former Goose Eye Brewery owner Bryan Fastell.

Old Brown aged ales from East Flanders.

Old Cannon Brewery Ltd. pub with brewery built in 1845 in Bury St Edmunds. Re-opened in 1999 with new plant.

Old Chimneys Brewery Norfolk craft brewery opened in 1995.

Old Laxey Brewing Co Ltd. Isle of Man brewery since 1997.

Old Luxters Vineyard Winery & Brewery Buckinghamshire brewery set up in 1990.

Old Mill Brewery Ltd. Yorkshire micro opened in 1983. A new brewhouse was installed in 1991 and a bottling plant in 1997.

Old Pint Pot Brewery Salford pub brewing since 1996.

Old Red aged ales from West Flanders.

Olde English 800 a strong beer brewed in the United States (7.5 per cent alcohol), by Blitz-Weinhard of Portland, Oregon.

Oldershaw Brewery home-based Lincolnshire brewery supplying local free houses.

Oldham Manchester brewery taken over in 1982 by neighbours, Boddingtons, famous for its OB Pale Ale.

Olympia a clean, light American beer from Olympia, Washington.

Omega high-bittering copper hop with an alpha acid content of 9.7%.

on draught beer available from the cask, not in a bottle.

op fles *(Dutch/Flemish)* in a bottle.

op gist *(Dutch/Flemish)* with yeast sediment.

opening times the times when licensed premises are permitted to sell alcohol. Prior to August 1988 the most common licensing hours in England and Wales were 10.30 a. m. to 2.30 p. m. and 5.30 to 10.30 p. m. (11 p. m. Fridays and Saturdays). Sunday 12 to 2 p. m. and 7 to 10.30 p. m. The weekday limit was 9 or 9 1/2 hours a day with a minimum two-hour break in the afternoon and a final closing time of 10.30 or 11 p. m. In August 1988 the government introduced all-day weekday opening in pubs. This followed a long campaign by CAMRA, which believed that the licensing hours were restrictive and that the licensee should be free to open any hours he/she chose. Scottish all-day opening showed the way. In 1995 Sunday afternoon opening was introduced.

Oranjeboom *(Dutch: "orange tree").* Dutch brewery in Rotterdam.

Orchard Brewery Bar Barnsley brew pub.

Orchard Brewery Lincolnshire micro.

Ordinary popular name for standard bitters when the Bitter is compared with the Special.

organic beer beer brewed from organically-grown ingredients. At present British brewers who produce organic beers have to source most of their ingredients from abroad.

Organic Brewhouse small Cornish brewery set up in 2000, dedicated to brewing organic real ales.

organic hops hops which are grown without the use of chemical pesticides or fertilizers. At present, most of the organic hops are imported from New Zealand. The only regular grower of organic hops in England is Peter Hall at Marden in Kent.

organic malt malt from barley which has been grown without the use of chemical pesticides or fertilizers. Organic malt has been previously imported from France and Germany.

orge *(French)* barley.

Original unoriginal name for usually stronger than average cask bitters.

original gravity *(brewing)* the British brewing industry's method of expressing the strength of beer. Pure water is defined as a gravity of 1000. Wort that is ready to start fermentation is denser than water, because of the fermentable material i.e. dissolved sugars. It is this density, the original gravity, which used to be measured to assess the excise duty. The higher the original gravity, the more fermentable material and thus a stronger finished beer. Most bitter beers have original gravities in the range 1035 to 1045, i.e. about 4% denser than water. Fermentation converts the sugars into alcohol, reducing the density of the liquid; at the end of the fermentation period the beer reaches its final gravity. Final gravities are normally in the region 1008-1015. The higher the figure, the sweeter the beer. Compare: alcohol by volume (ABV). Often the original gravity and the alcohol by volume of a beer are the same. A lower original gravity is an indication of a well attenuated beer. A higher original gravity is an indication of residual sugars remaining in the beer. Abbreviation: OG.

Orkney Brewery Ltd. set up in 1988 and modernised in 1995.

Orval distinctive triple-fermented Trappist beer (5.7 per cent alcohol) in an unusual skittle-shaped bottle, from the Abbaye of Orval in the far south of Belgium.

Ossett Brewing Company brewery at Brewers Pride pub in Yorkshire.

Österreichische Lebensmittelbuch (das) *(Austrian)* Codex Alimentarius Austriacus: the Austrian law which decrees which ingredients and additives are permitted in the brewing of beer.

Otter Brewery Ltd. mid-sized brewery operation since 1990. Devon based.

Oud Bruin Dutch table lagers containing less than 3.5 per cent abv and therefore very sweet.

Oudenaarde a Belgian town famous for its top-fermenting brown ales.

out of one's head *(slang)* description of someone who is drunk.

over-hopping the addition of too many hops, resulting in an acrid beer.

over-sparging the act of spraying too much hot water onto the mash before all the starch has been converted to sugars. As a result the beer will have a starch haze.

over-steep to prolong the steep, which can result in delayed germination.

oxidation any chemical reaction which involves oxygen. Detrimental to the flavour of beer.

oxidised *(beer evaluation)* having a cardboard-like aftertaste, which often occurs if the beer has been aerated during bottling and racking.

Oyster Stout popular name for a stout
   style beer.

P & DJ Goacher set up in 1983, Goacher's produces all-malt ales with only local Kentish hops.

Paasbier *(Dutch)* Easter beers.

Pacific Oriental brewery in restaurant, based in the heart of the City of London since 1998.

Packhorse Brewing Co Ltd.
Portsmouth brewery, risen from the ashes of the Ashford Brewery.

palate *(beer evaluation)* the sense of taste.

Palatinat Brewery Australian brewer brewing beers to the German purity law of 1516 (Deutsches Reinheitsgebot).

pale ale brewing ale style using light malts and Golding hops to produce a medium-gravity bottled ale, usually of about the same strength and hop rate as 'best bitter'. Some brewers produce a strong pale ale, of around 1045-1050 OG. In the southwest, pale ales are low-gravity draught beers.

pale amber *(beer evaluation)* a colour definition.

pale bok amber coloured, sweetish Dutch beer style.

pale lager international beer style, based loosely on the Pilsener style, with a 3.5-5% abv.

pale malt lightly kilned malted barley, with a pale colour (5 EBC). General term for ale malts (excluding coloured malts such as chocolate malt).

pale straw *(beer evaluation)* a colour definition.

Palmer partly thatched family brewery in a delightful seaside setting in Bridport, Dorset.

parachute *(brewing)* similar to a funnel that sits in the fermenting vessel at the level of the yeast head; excess yeast spills over into the parachute and is drawn off.

Paradise unusual brewery set up in a Cornish bird park in Hayle in 1981, behind the one tied house, the Bird in Hand.

paraflow *(brewing)* the heat-exchanger that cools the wort from the near boiling-point at which it leaves the copper down to fermenting temperature. A now generic term deriving from the paraflow which was originally marketed by APV.

paralytic *(slang)* description of someone who is drunk.

Parish Brewery began in 1982. Moved and expanded in 1992. Famous for brewing the strongest beer in the world, with an ABV of 23%, as listed in the Guinness Book of Records.

parlour the landlord's own bar room, usually a seating area behind the bar front, sometimes in the landlord's private quarters. Admission is traditionally by invitation only. Such bars are now scarce.

partial mashing *(brewing)* a method of brewing from diastatic malt extract, for which a mash tun is not required as all the ingredients are contained in the boiler. Before being raised to the boil, the temperature of the boiler is held at 67°Celsius (157°F) for 45 minutes.

parti-gyle *(brewing)* a variety of beers made from the same mash or to the same recipe, but which have had different quantities of water added at fermentation.

Passageway Brewing Company Liverpool brewery experiments with continental styles, since 1994.

pasteurisation heat treatment of filtered beer (bottled or keg) to kill off remaining yeast cells, leaving beer dead and sterile. Ensures that no further maturing can take place. Often gives the beer a 'cooked' flavour. The term derives from Pasteur, the French scientist, who pioneered fermentation and sterilisation. To satisfy CAMRA's definition of pure beer there should be no pasteurisation of the beer.

pasteurised beer beer which has been heat treated to prevent further fermentation.

Paulaner the Munich brewery which created two German lager styles: the powerful Doppelbock (own brand Salvator) and the pale Münchner.

Payn Breweries Ltd. built in Ramsey in 1999.

pbd *(abbreviation; Campaign)* progressive beer duty: a fair system of beer excise promoted by CAMRA, whereby the very small brewery companies (which have less than 2% of the beer market) would pay a lower rate of beer tax than the three brewing giants (which currently command approximately 85% of the beer market). In the March 2001 Budget, the Chancellor decided to 'freeze' the current excise duty on beer.

peardrops *(beer evaluation)* having a sweet, fruity aftertaste.

Peeterman an ungarnished version of the unique Belgian white beer, Hoegaards Wit, recreating the ancient beer style of Louvain.

peg *(slang)* a term for drink pertaining to the mediaeval practice of placing pegs in communal drinking flagons to ensure fair distribution of the contents.

Pelforth French brewery, based in Lille, famous for its top-fermenting beers, especially Pelforth Brune (1069), its strong brown ale.

pellets compacted hop cones.

Pembroke Brewery Co.
Pembrokeshire brewery started in 1994.

Perle a German general purpose/bittering hop. Also grown in the US. 7-9.5% alpha acid content.

P. E. T. *(abbreviation)* polyethylene terephthalate – a transparent, rigid plastic. P. E. T. bottles were introduced initially as large lemonade and cola containers but now are extensively used for beer, especially in supermarkets. Most common plastics are porous to carbon dioxide and so cannot be used for carbonated drinks. P. E. T. does not have this drawback and as a consequence has made large inroads into the glass bottle and can markets.

petite bière *(French: "small beer")* beer with an original gravity of not higher than 2° Régie.

Petty Sessions alternative term for a magistrates' court, which grants and refuses licence applications.

pewter an alloy of mostly tin with the addition of lead and sometimes copper and antimony. Formerly used for making the 'Pewter Pot' which was the standard pub drinking vessel until the 20th century. Nowadays, pewter mugs are mostly used for presentation purposes and as prizes for pub sports. Many locals have large collections of the regulars' private 'pewters', mostly illegal, as they are not government-stamped.

pH a measure of the acidity or alkalinity of a fluid. A measurement below 7 is acid; a measurement above 7 is alkaline.

phenolic flavour *(beer evaluation)* having a medicinal aftertaste, caused by the phenols produced during fermentation.

phenolic odour a plastic or chlorine smell to the beer, often caused by chlorinated water or brewing equipment, which has not been rinsed properly.

phenols volatile compounds in beer. Incorrect mash or sparging water temperatures can release phenols from the husks of the grain, resulting in phenolic odours.

Phoenix & Firkin Early Bruce homebrew pub which rose out of the ashes of Denmark Hill railway station, London.

Phoenix Brewery the trading name of Oak Brewing Co Ltd. and the original name of the brewery now inhabited. First established in 1982.

piccola *(Italian)* a standard 'small' glass of beer.

Picks Brewery in the cellar of the Red Lion Hotel, Accrington, Lancashire.

Pictish Brewing Company
Rochdale brewery established in 2000 by Richard Sutton, formerly senior brewer for the north with the Firkin Brewery.

piggin   a two-gallon cask. Rarely used today.

Pig's Ear   a London beer festival.

pig's ear   rhyming slang for beer.

Pilgrim Ales brewing since 1982. Moved to Reigate in 1985.

Pils   short for Pilsener, but in Britain used to refer to a specific type of strong bottled lager.

Pilsator   *(German)* a speciality beer from the former East Germany. It is not as dry as Pils and not as malty as Export.

Pilsener or Pilsner   a golden hoppy lager from light malt, soft water, bottom-fermented yeast and aroma hops, originating in the Czech town of Plzen (Pilsen in German) in 1842, and now loosely copied around the world. Traditionally it described a brewing process rather than a beer type. Typical Pilsener glasses have a bulb and are narrow at the top.

Pilsener malt   a light malt, which can make up to 100% of the grist. It can be used for brewing practically any beer. See also pale malt.

Pilsner Urquell the original – and best – Pilsener (5 per cent alcohol) from the Czech town of Plzen (Pilsen in German). Known in Bohemia as Plzensky Prazdroj, the beer is lagered in wooden casks for three months. Most British 'lagers' are lucky to get three weeks.

pin   a 4 1/2-gallon cask. Now uncommon, owing to the expense of breweries handling such small quantities. See polypin.

Pinkus Muller West German homebrew house in Münster, famous for its unusual wheat Altbier.

PINT *(abbreviation; Dutch)* Vereniging Promotie Informatie Traditioneel Bier: an organisation of Dutch beer lovers, founded in 1981 to promote real ale in the Netherlands.

pint   a standard Imperial measure (1/8 gallon) in a pub, equal to 20 fluid ounces. CAMRA supports the retention of the pint measure for draught beers and believes that appropriate Weights & Measures legislation should exist which defines a pint of beer as 20fl oz of liquid excluding any head of froth or foam.

Pioneer   a British general purpose hop with an alpha acid content of 10-11%.

pipkin   a party-sized tin of beer, usually containing about a gallon.

pissed   *(slang)* description of someone who is drunk.

pitch the widest diameter of a cask. Also known as bilge.

pitch (to) *(brewing)* to add yeast into the fermenting vessel. After the malted grain is mashed and the liquid (wort) is run off into fermenting vessels, the fermentation is started by the addition of yeast. In brewery terms, this is the pitching of the yeast.

Pitfield Brewery the first British brewery to be set up in an off licence (the Beer Shop in Hoxton, North London). Its beers are brewed from organic ingredients and its Hallertauer hops are imported from New Zealand. In 1988 its Dark Star (now Black Eagle) won the overall Champion Beer of Britain title.

pivnice *(Czech)* pub.

pivo *(Czech)* beer.

pivovar *(Czech)* brewery.

plain *(Irish)* a reference to Porter or Stout (particularly Guinness).

Plassey Brewery Wrexham brewery founded in 1985 in a leisure park.

Plato a saccharometer to measure the specific gravity. See degrees Plato; degrees Balling.

Plato a measure on the Plato saccharometer. Abbreviation: °P.

play for the gallon an expression in pub games where each losing team member has to buy a drink for his opponent.

Plough Inn & Leith Hill Brewery Surrey brewery started in 1996.

ploughman's a pub lunch; usually cold meats and/or cheese with pickle and salad.

plumule an alternative term for acrospire, the embryonal barley plant within the husk.

Plzen Czech Pilsner.

Plzensky Prazdroj *(Czech)* the original Pilsner from the Czech town of Plzen.

pocket *(brewing)* brewers' term for the sack used for packaging pressed and dried hop cones.

poisson poché à la bière *(French; culinary)* poached fish with beer.

polish (to) *(brewing)* the fine filtering of a light-coloured beer to make it brilliant and crystal-clear before bottling or kegging.

Polyclar a type of plastic, used to reduce chill haze.

polyethylene terephthalate a transparent, rigid plastic. The bottles made from this plastic were introduced initially as large (1.5 litre) lemonade and cola containers but now are extensively used for beer, especially in supermarkets. Unlike other common plastics, polyethylene terephthalate is not porous to carbon dioxide. Abbreviation: P. E. T.

polypin a plastic bag, inside a rigid cardboard container, holding about 4 1/2 gallons of beer. The mainstay of the take-home party trade.

pony beer glass size, usually 1/3 pint, usually given as a taster.

Poorter   *(Flemish)* a strong, dark, top-fermented speciality beer in Belgium, sold in a stoneware bottle.

Poperinge the vast hop-growing region of West Flanders.

Poperinge Hop Festival beer-drinking carnival held at Poperinge every three years.

porc à la bière *(French; culinary)* pork with beer.

porter a dark, slightly sweetish but hoppy ale made with roasted barley; the successor of 'entire' and predecessor of stout. Porter originated in London around 1730, and by the end of the 18th century was probably the most popular beer in England. It was usually matured in vast vats, and in 1814, when a porter vat at Meux's London brewery in Tottenham Court Road burst, the resulting flood of nearly 130,000 gallons of ale drowned eight people. The fashion for the pale ales of Burton-upon-Trent ended the popularity of porter in the mid-19th century. In recent years, a number of brewers have revived porter.

Porter Brewing Co Ltd. brews at the Rossendale Brewery at the Griffin Inn. Opened in 1994.

Porterhouse Dublin brewpub serving real ales and stout. Also in London (Covent Garden).

posset a hot drink made from sweetened milk curdled with ale and flavoured with spices.

posthumulone an alpha acid.

pot a 1/2 pint or full pint glass with a handle.

Potton Brewery Company run by ex-managers of Greene King at Biggleswade.

Pottsville Porter a dark 'roasted' beer (5 per cent alcohol) from the USA's oldest brewers, Yuengling of Pennsylvania. Such brews demonstrate the East Coast's British ale heritage.

POTY *(abbreviation; Campaign)* Pub of the Year. A competition held annually to recognise and reward excellence amongst British pubs and to generate positive publicity both for CAMRA and for pubs.

powdery mildew a hop disease caused by parasitic fungi.

precipitation *(brewing)* the "dropping out" of particles from solution.

prehumulone an alpha acid.

Premium a name used for any stronger-than-average beer.

Pride of Ringwood an Australian general purpose/bittering hop, giving a citrus aroma.

primary fermentation *(brewing)* the initial stage of fermentation during which the fermentable sugars are converted to ethyl alcohol and carbon dioxide in the brewery fermentation vessels. The process applies to all beers, traditional or processed, although, in order to satisfy CAMRA's definition of pure beer, the primary fermentation should be effected with a top fermenting yeast.

prime (to) *(brewing)* to add of a small quantity of sugar to each cask of certain beers as the cask is filled. This priming with priming sugar encourages the secondary fermentation and adds some sweetness and colour. Excise regulations require a special licence for premises where priming is conducted.

Prince of Wales Cumbrian brewery attached to the Prince of Wales inn.

Princetown Breweries Ltd. Devon brewery established in 1994 by a former Gibbs Mew and Hop Back brewer.

Privat *(German)* another name for Export.

prodotto dalla *(Italian)* brewed by.

Progress a British aroma hop with an alpha acid content of 5-6%.

progressive beer duty *(Campaign)* a fair system of beer excise promoted by CAMRA, whereby the very small brewery companies (which have less than 2% of the beer market) would pay a lower rate of beer tax than the three brewing giants (which currently command approximately 85% of the beer market). In the March 2001 Budget, the Chancellor decided to 'freeze' the current excise duty on beer. Abbreviation: pbd.

Prohibition a law which came into force in January,1920 in USA and which forbade the production, sale, import and transportation of alcoholic beverages in the USA. The law was repealed 13 years later.

Propylene glycol alginate *(brewing)* a commercial preparation for head retention. Derived from alginic acid from seaweed.

prost *(German)* cheers!

protein any complex organic compound containing nitrogen.

psenicove pivo *(Czech)* wheat beer.

pub a house open to the public at stated times for the purpose of social drinking – Britain's greatest social institution.

pub chain a group of pubs owned by a management company specifically set up to manage an estate. Ownership varies from a few pubs in a single town to hundreds on a national scale.

pub group a company that owns and runs a large number of pubs, but does not brew. In the UK brewers have sold many of their pubs to such groups.

Pub of the Year *(Campaign)* a competition held annually to recognise and reward excellence amongst British pubs and to generate positive publicity both for CAMRA and for pubs. Abbreviation: POTY.

public bar the basic drinking bar of a pub, with the emphasis on games like darts and dominoes rather than soft furnishings. Increasingly threatened by pub 'improvements'.

Public House Viability Test *(Campaign)* a campaigning initiative by CAMRA which seeks to offer planning authorities a clear and objective checklist of relevant factors on which they can come to an objective decision on granting or refusing planning permission to owners of country pubs who wish to convert them into private houses on the grounds that they are no longer viable as businesses.

publican the keeper of a public house. Also called host, landlord, licensee.

pumpclip a mini sign attached to the front of the handpump which advertises the name of the beer on offer. CAMRA believes that the clip should be turned behind the pump if the beer in question is not available.

puncheon a 72-gallon cask, now only of historic interest.

pundy a Scottish term, dating from the 17th century, for second mash, low-gravity beer, also known as small beer. Term replaced by 'table beer' in the late 19th century. The term has also been used to describe the free allowance of beer issued to brewery workers. See also Strong Ale.

Purity Law the German Reinheitsgebot of 1516, which rigidly decreed that the only ingredients which may be used in the brewing of beer were water, barley or wheat, hops and yeast. Chemical additives, widely used in the British commercial brewing industry, were banned. Even sugar was not not allowed. In 1993 new beer tax legislation came into force, which superseded the Purity Law. Thus the use of additives etc. by brewers is now permitted, although the Purity Law remains the benchmark of quality and is still commercial practice.

Python *(brewing)* a type of hose. Generically used to refer, in a cellar, to beer lines enclosed within a sheath which also contains the refrigeration pipe.

quaff (to) to drink heartily.

quaffable easy to drink in quantity.

quality   the classification of beer styles e.g. mild, bitter, best bitter.

quart a liquid measure equal to two Imperial pints (a quarter of a gallon). Until the early part of this century, a common size of serving mug.

quarter   a standard measure of barley (448 lbs) as bought by the maltster. Each quarter should yield about 336 lbs of malt and in turn yield 80-100 lbs of extract for the brewer.

quarter   the side of the cask between the chimb and the bilge.

quartern   a gill, equivalent to 1/4 Imperial pint.

Quay Brewery   a Weymouth brewery set up in summer 1996 in the old Devenish and Groves brewery buildings. The brewery is independent and is open to visitors as part of the Timewalk attraction.

race (to) *(brewing)* to ferment too rapidly. If the temperature at which fermentation takes place is too high, fermentation may race, producing coarse flavours.

rack (to) *(brewing)* to transfer beer from a tank to a cask or keg. CAMRA believes that all casks should be clearly labelled with the racking date of the beer.

racking back *(brewing)* term applied to storing green beer in a tank for a short time before its transferral, or 'racking' to a barrel.

racking gravity *(brewing)* the specific gravity at which green beer is transferred from a tank to a barrel.

racking line in a brewery, where the beer is transferred from a tank to a cask or keg.

Radler a Bavarian beer and lemonade mix.

railway taverns inns, built to cater for the railway travellers, which superseded the coaching inns during the rise of the railways during the nineteenth century.

Rainbow Inn & Brewery Coventry brewery since 1994.

Rainier an American ale of distinction, from Seattle, Washington, known as the Green Death because of its green label and high alcohol content (7.25 per cent).

rake *(brewing)* a rotating arm which can be attached to the base of a mash tun to thoroughly mix the mash.

Randall Guernsey's smaller brewery in St Peter Port. Not related to Randalls Vautier.

Rat & Ratchet Brewery Huddersfield alehouse where beer has been brewed since 1994.

Rauchbier *(German: "smoke beer")* the dark 'smoked' beers of Bamberg, Bavaria, which are produced from malt which has been fire-dried over beechwood logs. This gives the resulting 1055 brew a distinctive roasted flavour. The best-known brand is Kaiserdom but the most memorable is from the Schlenkerla homebrew house.

raw grain *(brewing)* any grain besides malt. See adjuncts.

Rayment former Hertfordshire brewery taken over and shut by Greene King.

RCH Brewery brewing since 1993 in a former cider mill at West Hewish. Active since early 1980s.

Reading Lion Brewery brewery opened by Hop Back Brewery in 1995 at the Hop Leaf pub.

Real Ale *(Campaign)* beer brewed from traditional ingredients, matured by secondary fermentation in the container from which it is dispensed, and served without the use of extraneous carbon dioxide; also called 'cask-conditioned' and 'naturally conditioned' beer. Name and definition coined by CAMRA, the Campaign for Real Ale.

Real Ale in a Bottle beer which continues to ferment, mature and condition within the bottle. It contains a visible amount of viable yeast cells together with sufficient fermentable sugars for this to take place.

Real Ale Fighting Fund *(Campaign)* fund-raising activities and donations are made to a specific fund for raising awareness of real ale through the 'Ask if it's Cask' campaign. Members and branches organise raffles, competitions and other fund-raising activities in addition to their normal campaigning.

Rebellion Beer Company   based in Marlow, Bucks. The brewery fills the gap left in Marlow by Whitbread, which shut down Wethereds in 1988.

Rectory Ales Ltd. founded in 1996 by the Rector of Plumpton (Sussex), the Rev Godfrey Broster, to generate funds for the maintenance of the three churches in his parish. To date107 parishioners are shareholders.

Red Shoot Brewery   H a m p s h i r e brewery since 1998 when Forest Gold was the first brew.

red spider mite serious orchard pest.

Red Stripe the West Indies' best-known lager, from Jamaica.

Red Witch a beer cocktail made with stout, Pernod, cider and blackcurrant.

Redruth Brewery (1742) Ltd. Cornish brewery which has been brewing cask-conditioned beer since 1998.

reekin'   Scottish slang for 'smelling of drink'.

Reepham Brewery Norfolk   family-owned micro-brewery started in 1983.

refermentation a secondary fermentation.

refermentée en bouteille   *(French)* bottle fermented/conditioned.

refrigerator *(brewing)* a wort cooler.

Régie a scale of measurement used in France to measure the original gravity of the wort. See degrees Régie. Abbreviation: °R.

Reinheitsgebot German beer Purity Law, dating from 1516, which rigidly decreed that the only ingredients permitted in the brewing of beer were water, barley or wheat, hops, and yeast. Chemical additives, widely used in the British brewing industry, were banned. Even sugar was not allowed. In 1993 new beer tax legislation came into force, which superseded the Purity Law. Thus the use of additives etc. by brewers is permitted, although the

Reinheitsgebot remains the benchmark of quality and is still commercial practice.

Resch's KB an Australian lager produced by Tooths of Sydney.

respiration *(brewing)* the chemical breakdown of complex organic substances to release energy.

Restalrig Village Brewery Ltd. Edinburgh brewery setup in 1997 in an old woollen mill.

retorrefication *(brewing)* the traditional practice of gently heating the grist before it is added to the mash tun. A similar process is used in some modern mills (steam modification).

Rezani *(Czech)* mixed beer (half pale, half dark).

rhizomes the shoots of the hop plant which run a few centimetres underground and emerge as new plants after root cutting.

Ridley & Sons Ltd. Essex brewery established by Thomas Dixon Ridley in 1842 and still family run. Still produces fine, good-value 'beers from the wood'. Won the first ever CAMRA beer award at the exhibition at Alexandra Palace in 1978, for its PA bitter.

right arm *(slang)* term for drinking, as in 'exercise my right arm'. The lever used to raise the glass to the lips (except in left-handed drinkers!).

Ringwood Brewery Ltd. Hampshire micro set up in 1978 by one of the fathers of the new brewery movement, Peter Austin. Now based in what was formerly part of the old Tunks brewery. Much expanded over the years.

Ritchie Bruheat *(homebrewing)* a purpose-built, polypropylene boiler.

Riverhead Brewery Ltd. Huddersfield brew pub that opened in 1995.

road house a large pub of the inter-war period catering for motor car and coach trade, particularly at the outer edges of large urban areas and along arterial roads. On the advent of the breathalyser, these road houses were converted apace to steakhouses etc.

roast *(beer evaluation)* having a coffee-like character from dark and roasted malts.

roasted barley *(brewing)* kilned unmalted barley, dark in colour (1000-1550 EBC), used mainly to add colour and, because of its beta glucans, head to stouts and porters.

roasted malt see chocolate malt.

Robinson's Stockport family brewery founded in 1838. In 1982 it took over Hartleys of Cumbria. One of the few breweries still using wooden casks.

Rochefort the third Belgian Trappist Abbaye brewery in the foothills of the Ardennes, producing a similar range of beers to Chimay.

Rockingham Ales part-time Northants micro-brewery established in 1997.

Rodenbach a Belgian soured ale.

rogge *(Dutch)* rye.

Roggen *(German)* rye.

Roggenbier *(German)* bottom-fermented rye beer using rye malt instead of barley malt.

rolling boil *(brewing)* a rolling (or vigorous boil), essential for ideal wort production.

Roosters Brewing Co Ltd. Harrogate micro since 1993, run by Sean and Alison Franklin.

rope *(brewing)* a bacterial infection of beer, much dreaded by the brewer. The infective agent is an anaerobic bacterium called Zymamonas, whose action produces slimy gelatinous threads in the beer – a cask can be completely ruined in a matter of hours. 'Ropey' beer has given the language the general slang expression for 'of bad or poor quality'. Easily controlled by scrupulous hygiene as well as clean casks and efficient cask washers.

rossa *(Italian: "red")* a bitter-style beer.

Rother Valley Brewing Company established in Northiam, Sussex in 1993 on a hop farm overlooking the river that marks the boundary between Kent and Sussex.

rotten *(slang)* description of someone who is drunk.

round the buying of drinks by one person for everyone in the group.

rouse (to) *(brewing)* to stir or mix. For example, fermenting wort may be roused from time to time: traditionally with large wooden paddles but now more commonly by injection of air bubbles, or by recycling the wort – pumping it in a fan-shaped spray back across the yeast head.

rouser *(homebrewing)* a brewer's paddle.

rowan ale ale using rowan berries as the principal flavouring.

rubidy also rubbity or rubberdy. Australian term for a pub. Derives from rhyming slang rubadubdub.

Ruddles one of the most famous real ale brewers, from Rutland, Leicestershire. In 1977 the Langham family firm sold its 37 pubs to finance expansion of the brewery, to supply packaged beer to supermarkets and its celebrated County to the free trade. The brewery was taken over, resold and eventually closed: a tragic fate applicable to many similar breweries around the UK.

Rudgate Brewery Ltd. North Yorks brewery founded in 1992, located in an old armoury building on a disused airfield.

running bead the constant stream of bubbles rising up from the bottom to the surface of the beer.

running off *(brewing)* the act of emptying the mash tun or other vessel.

runnings *(brewing)* the wort which drains from the mash tun.

rural inn an alternative name for a country pub. Country pubs in the UK are currently closing at the rate of six a week. CAMRA believes that country pubs are essential community amenities and should be eligible to receive 50% mandatory relief on their business rates. The government passed a bill in 2001 providing a 50% reduction on business rates to sole pubs in settlements with fewer than 3,000 in habitants and with a rateable value below £9,000.

Russian Stout remarkable, powerful bottle-conditioned stout, reputedly made popular by Empress Catherine the Great and originally produced by London brewers for export to the Baltic.

RW Randall Ltd. Guernsey brewery in St Peter Port.

Ryburn Brewery West Yorks brewery founded in 1989 in a former dye works.

rye a hardy cereal and its grain.

rye beer a German beer style using rye malt instead of barley malt and using the bottom fermented method of brewing.

rye malt rye which has been partially germinated and then kilned.

SA Brain & Company Ltd. a traditional brewery which started trading under the Brain name in 1882. Leading pub owner and brewer based in Cardiff, Wales.

Saaz the internationally revered aroma hops, with an alpha acid content of 3-3.5%, from the Czech region of Bohemia, centred on the town of Zatec. Delicate, floral aroma for Czech-style lagers.

saccharification *(brewing)* the conversion of starch into sugar during the mashing process.

saccharimeter *(brewing)* an instrument used to measure sugar concentrations by changes in optical properties.

saccharometer *(brewing)* an instrument used to measure the sugar content of the wort; also called a hydrometer.

Saccharomyces scientific name for yeast.

Saccharomyces carlsbergensis scientific name for bottom-fermenting yeast.

Saccharomyces cerevisiae a top-fermenting ale yeast.

Saccharomyces delbrueckii a strain of wheat yeast, used in Bavarian Weizenbier (wheat beer).

Saccharomyces uvarum (formerly Saccharomyces carlsbergensis) a bottom-fermenting lager yeast.

sack *(brewing)* brewers' term for the plastic or hessian container used for packaging malt.

safe drinking safe limits of alcohol consumption: there is insufficient scientific evidence to state categorically how much alcohol an individual can consume without damaging effects. However, the medical profession generally defines safe levels as up to 21 units a week for men and up to 14 units a week for women. Dangerous levels are defined as above 49 units a week for men and 35 units a week for women.

Sahti *(Finnish)* traditional home-brew beer, flavoured with juniper berries.

saison Wallonian top-fermenting, bottle-conditioned pale ales, traditionally brewed in the spring and presented in Champagne-style bottles.

sake japanese rice beer.

Saladin boxes *(malting)* huge, uncovered, open-ended, rectangular boxes used for modifying barley during the malting process. Also called germination boxes. See also Wanderhausen.

saloon essentially the same as the lounge, a pub room which is more comfortably furnished than the public bar.

Salopian Brewing brewery started in 1995 in an old dairy on the outskirts of Shrewsbury.

salty *(beer evaluation)* having a saline aftertaste, caused primarily if the water supply has a high salt content or if too much brewing salt has been used.

Salvator the very first German Doppelbock or 'double bock' beer, now produced by the Paulaner brewery of Munich.

Sam Trueman's Brewery Trueman's brews for the Crown & Anchor in Marlow.

Samichlaus one of the world's strongest beers, brewed by Hurlimann of Switzerland, containing 14 per cent alcohol. 'Santa Claus' does not start with the highest original gravity (1102), but is lagered for a whole year to produce its mighty strength.

sam-shu Chinese rice beer.

Samuel Smith Old Brewery (Tadcaster) Yorkshire's oldest brewery, dating from 1758. Related to the nearby much larger John Smith's but still family-owned and brewing with tradition.

sans produits chimiques *(French)* without chemical additives.

Sanwald Stuttgart brewers specialising in German Weizen (wheat) beers.

Sarah Hughes Brewery re-opened by John Hughes in 1987 to reproduce grandmother's Dark Ruby beer. Originally founded in the 1860s.

Scaldis strongest Belgian speciality beer (12% abv) similar to barley wine. Also called Bush Beer.

Scattor Rock Brewery Ltd. set up in 1998 within the boundaries of the Dartmoor National Park.

Schaapskooi the only Dutch Trappist brewery, producing the bottle-conditioned ale, La Trappe, from the abbey near Tilburg.

Schankbier *(German)* a category of beer in Germany which includes all beers with between 2.5 and 3.7% abv.

Schlenkerla a German homebrew tavern in Bamberg, Bavaria, dating back to 1678, and producing the most intense of the town's famous Rauchbiere (smoked beers).

Schlitz the beer that made Milwaukee famous, once the largest brewing company in America. Then the quality of its product slipped and so did its standing. Today the Milwaukee brewery is closed, the company having been taken over by rivals Stroh.

Schneider a Bavarian wheat double bock and a Bavarian wheat beer.

Schultheiss Berlin's major brewery, known for its Weisse (white) beer. With Dortmunder Union, it forms one of the largest brewing groups in Germany.

Scotch ale a term more in use in the northeast of England than in Scotland, referring to 'heavy' ale. In Belgium scotch ale means a strong, dark, bottled beer. There are also strong 'Christmas Ales' under the same name.

scotches chocks.

Scottish & Newcastle brewing and retail group that comprises Scottish Courage (UK), Brasseries Kronenbourg (France), Alken Maes (Belgium) and Scottish & Newcastle Retail. The company can trace its roots back to 1749, when the William Younger Brewery was established in Leith. Acquired Greenalls in 1999. Has a joint venture to run the Portuguese brewer and distributor Central De Cervejas.

Scottish air pressure system a traditional beer dispense system which involves the application of compressed air onto the surface of the beer in the cask, forcing the beer up to the counter through an extractor syphon. As the term implies, the system is little-used in England but still used in Scotland, where it operates in conjunction with tall founts.

Scottish Brewers Scottish arm of Scottish & Newcastle formed in 1931 through the merger of Edinburgh brewers, William Younger and McEwan. A new brewery was built on McEwan's Fountainbridge site in 1974.

Scottish Courage brewer formed in 1995, following Scottish & Newcastle's acquisition of Courage. It has seven breweries – six in the UK and Beamish & Crawford in Eire. It also has interests in maltings through Bairds Malt.

Scottish Hours Scottish pub opening hours, which were formerly restricted, although 'regular extension' licences allowed pubs to remain open beyond the restrictions. Thus, the actual hours varied a great deal within each region according to the whims of the licensing boards. The licensing arrangement was often referred to as the 'Scottish Experiment' and paved the way for all-day opening.

Scura *(Italian)* a 'Guinness' style beer.

secondary fermentation *(brewing)* a further fermentation which allows any remaining fermentable sugars to be converted to ethyl alcohol and carbon dioxide. After the primary fermentation, beers that are to be cask-conditioned are racked into the casks together with some residual yeast. This yeast continues a slow secondary fermentation in the cask – all-important if the beer's full flavour is to develop. True lagers also have a secondary fermentation but in large refrigerated tanks known as lagering tanks. Secondary fermentation is an essential and indispensable characteristic of real ale and should continue for a period of at least seven days (in cask) before fining to satisfy CAMRA's definition of pure beer.

sediment the sludgy material that settles out of cask-conditioned beer by the action of the finings. It consists mostly of dead yeast cells but also contains some proteins, and some hops if the cask was dry hopped. Also known as lees.

seigle *(French)* rye.

Selby (Middlesbrough) Brewery Ltd. family brewery that resumed brewing in 1972.

Sensible Modicum immortalised phrase following the trial for drunk-driving of a Scottish judge, who said in his defence that he had consumed only a 'sensible modicum' of whisky.

session *(slang)* an alcohol-inspired get-together.

set mash *(brewing)* an occasional problem with a mash where the whole mixture becomes very sticky and the wort will not drain off properly.

70/-Ale Scottish term for medium-gravity beers. Usually 1034-1039 and light in colour. The term is synonymous with 'heavy' in Scotland. See shilling system.

SG *(abbreviation)* specific gravity: a measure of the density of a liquid or solid as compared to that of water. Expressed as a ratio.

shandy a half-and-half mixture of beer and lemonade. Bottled shandy is virtually non-alcoholic. See Radler.

Shardlow Brewing Company Ltd. brewery opened in 1993 in the old kiln house of the original Cavendish Bridge Brewery.

Sharps Brewery founded in 1994, the brewery has enjoyed rapid expansion in Devon and Cornwall.

sheaf the barley sheaf is a popular symbol for British breweries and pub signs.

Sheffield Stout a beer cocktail made with black beer and lemonade. See black beer.

shelf life the length of time a beer can be kept without deteriorating. See also antioxidant.

Shepherd Neame Ltd. Kent's major independent brewery. There are records of brewing on the Faversham site since the 12th century. The same water source is still used today, steam engines are deployed and the mash is produced in two teak tuns that date from 1910. A campaigner for lower tax on beer because of the detrimental import of European beers via the channel tunnel.

shilling system a code of beer grading used in Scotland. The system of marking beers 70/-, 80/-, etc, was first used in the 1870s as the gross invoice price for a barrel of beer (net price was always different as it included discounts and sundry costs), i.e. an 80/- ale would never actually cost the publican 80 shillings (or £4 in today's money). Because of the progressive beer duty levied in Britain, where higher gravity beers are taxed more, the higher the shilling mark, the stronger the beer. An 80/-beer would always be stronger than a 60/- beer. CAMRA believes that the shilling system should only be used for cask conditioned products and should not be used for keg beers.

shive a wooden or nylon bung, several inches in diameter, fitted to casks and used to stop up the bung hole through which the cask is filled. A small central piece of the shive (the tut) is knocked through to vent the cask via the spile hole.

shive bush traditionally a brass, but now a plastic insert in wooden barrels to hold the bung in place.

Shoes Brewery Hereford brew pub since 1994.

Shoreditch 1850 Porter a cask-conditioned organic beer, brewed by Pitfield (London).

short measure not a full half or pint measure, when dispensed. CAMRA supports the retention of the pint and half pint measures for draught beers and believes that appropriate Weights & Measures legislation should exist which defines a pint of beer as 20fl oz (a half pint as 10fl oz) of liquid excluding any head of froth or foam.

shout *(slang)* a round of drinks.

Shraley Brook Brewing Company Rising Sun Brewery revived by pub locals.

Siegel the Pils brand from the German giant, Dortmunder Union.

Sigl an Austrian wheat beer.

Six Bells Brewery brewing in Shropshire since 1997.

six-pack popular term for a take-home pack of bottled or canned beer.

six-rowed barley barleycorns that grow in six-rowed ears, more common outside the UK, especially in the USA. Compare two-rowed barley.

60/-Ale Scottish term for mild beers. Usually 1030-1034 and dark in colour. Synonymous with 'Light' in Scotland. See shilling system.

skål *(Danish)* cheers!

skim (to) *(brewing)* to remove periodically the excess yeast from the wort at the top of the fermenting vessel.

Much of this surplus yeast goes to make yeast extracts such as 'Marmite'.

skinful *(slang)* consumption of a large amount of beer.

Skinners Brewery brewery founded in 1997 by Steve and Sarah Skinner, formerly of the Tipsy Toad Brewery in Jersey.

sklep *(Czech)* cellar.

skull-dragged *(Irish)* to be hungover.

slate square *(brewing)* a traditional form of fermenting vessel, square in shape and formerly made of stone or slate slabs. New ones tend to be stainless steel. The top is partially covered in, with a central hole to allow the escape of yeast and carbon dioxide. Originally more common in the north, but now dying out for economic reasons. They are also known as squares or Yorkshire squares.

sleeve a straight glass without a handle. Also known as sleever.

slummage the sediment at the bottom of casks and fermentation vessels.

small beer a Scottish term for second mash, low-gravity beer, also known as pundy. See strong ale.

small beer someone or something of no importance (possibly deriving from the now rare term 'small beer' = weak beer).

smashed *(slang)* description of someone who is drunk.

Smiles Brewing Co Ltd. a traditional tower brewery founded in Bristol in 1977.

smoke room the forerunner of the lounge, especially in the north of England. Originally a room where customers retired to smoke.

smoked beer the dark beers of Bamberg, Bavaria, which are produced from malt which has been fire-dried over beechwood logs. This gives the resulting 1055 brew a distinctive roasted flavour. The best-known brand is Kaiserdom but the most memorable is from the Schlenkerla homebrew house. See Rauchbier.

smokey *(beer evaluation)* having a burnt, smokey flavour due to the use of peated malts.

smoothflow nitrokeg: keg beer which is dispensed with a mix of carbon dioxide and nitrogen. CAMRA affirms that nitrokeg is just another form of brewery conditioned/keg beer and condemns the excessive hype surrounding such beers, which are not real ales.

snob screen a pivoted decorated screen above the bar counter, designed (in Victorian pubs) to allow 'the elite' to drink in private.

Snowdonia Parc Brewery   b r e w - pub in the stationmaster's house for the Welsh Highland Railway since 1998.

snug a small room or a bar in a UK pub offering intimate seating for a few people; nowadays usually knocked through into larger bars.

social drinker a person who stays within the safe limits of alcohol consumption and who does not become intoxicated. See safe drinking.

Society for the Preservation of Beers from the Wood *(Campaign)* the former name of the consumer campaign CAMRA.

sodium chloride salt, a mineral sometimes added to water for brewing as a flavour enhancer, particularly for brown ales and stouts. Formula: NaCl.

soft lambic clear, filtered, sweetened lambic.

soft resins the alpha acids and beta acids in the lulupin. When the hops are boiled the bittering substances from the alpha and beta acids are extracted. Also called bitter resins.

soft spile a porous wooden peg, which is inserted into the shive to control the carbon dioxide content of the beer during a slow secondary fermentation.

soft water water which is relatively free of mineral salts (gypsum and magnesium). Not suited to ale brewing.

solvent   *(beer evaluation)* having a pungent aftertaste, often the result of the fermentation temperature being too high and producing esters and higher alcohols. Some wild yeasts and bacteria also cause solvent flavours.

sommelier   *(French: "butler")*. More traditionally a wine waiter, but can apply to knowledgeable servers of beer.

Sorghum beer an African 'wild' beer.

soul of beer a reference to malt.

soupe à la bière *(French; culinary)* beer soup.

sour *(beer evaluation)* having an acidic aftertaste, usually caused by an acetic acid bacteria or lactobacillus contamination.

sour beers the tart, acidic beers of Flanders.

SP Sporting Ales Ltd.   Hereford brewery since 1996.

Spalt Select a German aroma hop variety with an alpha acid content of 4.5-5%. Slightly spicy aroma.

sparge (to) *(brewing)* to spray hot liquor on to the top of the grains to flush out the last fermentables. This is done after the first strong worts are drawn off, as the wort is drawn off the mash. Usually the spray is from rotating, perforated tubes called sparge arms.

sparkler a device attached to the beer engine outlet. The beer is forced through very small holes to aerate it and produce a creamy 'tight head'. The amount of aeration can be varied: screwed up for a creamy head or screwed out for a 'flat' pint. CAMRA believes that beers should not be dispensed through a tight sparkler if they have not been brewed to be dispensed in that style.

Sparkling Ale a term historically used by brewers to indicate that their bottled beer was filtered.

Spaten a pioneer lager brewery, Spaten of Munich, which developed both the dark Münchner beer and the stronger Märzenbier. Its Münchner Dunkel Export (5 per cent alcohol) and Ur-Märzen (5.8) are classics of their styles.

special term to describe beer. Used at the maker's discretion and therefore not always applicable.

spéciale *(French)* special.

specific gravity a measure of the density of a liquid (or solid) as compared to that of water. Expressed as a ratio. Abbreviation: SG.

spent grains *(brewing)* brewers' term for left-over malt grains after mashing. Usually sold for cattle fodder.

spiced ale usually stronger pale and brown ales to which spices (coriander, cinnamon or ginger) have been added. See Christmas ales.

spicy *(beer evaluation)* having an aromatic cinnamon or cloves flavour, determined by the type of hop. A term often applied to lagers.

spigot the tapered end of a cask tap or tail.

spile a small wooden peg, which is inserted into the vent hole (shive) at the top of the cask while the conditioning beer is undergoing a secondary fermentation. A soft spile is porous and allows the excess carbon dioxide to escape slowly; a hard spile is used to seal the cask completely after venting or when not in service (to prevent entry of air or loss of too much gas).

spingo collective name of the beers brewed at the Blue Anchor, Helston, Cornwall.

Spinning Dog Brewery Hereford brewery opened in January 2000.

spoiled beer beer that has in some way become unfit for consumption while still at the brewery and on which the excise duty will be reclaimed.

spontaneous fermentation the fermentation of the mash by wild, airborne yeasts. See lambic.

Springhead Brewery started out as the country's smallest brewery but moved to larger premises in 1994.

square *(brewing)* a traditional form of fermenting vessel, square in shape and formerly made of stone or slate slabs. New ones tend to be stainless steel. The top is partially covered in, with a central hole to allow the escape of yeast and carbon dioxide. Originally more common in the north, but now dying out for economic reasons, they are often known as Yorkshire squares or slate squares.

SRM *(abbreviation)* Standard Research (or Reference) Method: a standard measurement of the colour range of a specific beer or beer style, used in the United States. The measurement can be given in degrees Lovibond (°L). See EBC. Conversion calculations: EBC = SRM x 1.97. SRM = EBC / 1.97.

St Arnould a bière de garde from France.

St Austell Brewery Co Ltd. brewing in the town since 1851, the present brewery dates from the early 1890s.

St George's Brewery Worcestershire brewery since 1998.

St Georges Brewing Co Ltd. brewing at the Saddleworth Brewery, Church Inn, Saddleworth.

St James's Gate Guinness brewery in Dublin, reputed to be the largest brewery in Europe.

St Leonard a French bière de garde (laying-down beer), from Boulogne.

St Peters Brewery Co Ltd. Suffolk company opened in 1996 in former dairy buildings behind the ancient St Peter's Hall in Bungay.

St Sixtus Abbaye at Westvleteren which produces the strongest beer in Belgium, Abt, with 12 per cent alcohol, in addition to two other Trappist beers. As the abbey brewery is small, the beers for public sale are brewed to the same recipe by the nearby commercial brewery, St Bernardus.

stale *(beer evaluation)* having a cardboard-like aftertaste, which often occurs if the beer has been aerated during bottling and racking.

Standard Reference Method a standard measurement of the colour range of a specific beer or beer style, used by the American Society of Brewing Chemists (ASBC) in the United States, indicated by degrees Lovibond (°L). Abbreviation: SRM. See EBC. Conversion calculations: EBC = SRM x 1.97. SRM = EBC / 1.97.

Standard Research Method see Standard Reference Method. Abbreviation: SRM.

Stanway Brewery G l o u c e s t e r s h i r e brewery founded in 1993.

star bright *(beer evaluation)* a term describing the absolute clarity of a beer.

Starkbier *(German: "strong beer")*. A category of beer in Germany which includes all beers with a minimum strength of 6.2% abv.

starting specific gravity the original gravity.

statutory consultation *(Campaign)* a campaigning initiative by CAMRA to secure for local CAMRA branches a place on local authorities' lists of statutory consultees on planning matters regarding any proposal to close a pub.

stave the curved wooden planks which make up the body of a cask.

steam beer a rare Californian method of brewing, using bottom-fermenting lager yeasts at ale temperatures. See Anchor Steam.

steam jackets *(brewing)* a modification of steam coils by which 'jackets' are fitted to the side of a copper and steam pumped into them to boil the wort. The term can also be used for any 'jacket' fitted to a tank.

steam modification *(brewing)* a pre-milling treatment of malt which softens the grain and causes partial gelatinisation of the starch. Compare retorrefication.

steaming *(slang)* a description of someone who is drunk.

Steel's masher *(brewing)* a rotary mixing device which ensures a correct balance of grist and liquor at the predetermined strike heat, and runs the mixture into the mash tun. Patented in 1853.

steep *(malting)* the water-absorption stage of the malting process, at which the barley is allowed to soak in water prior to germination.

Stein *(German: "stone")* a German drinking vessel, similar to an earthenware tankard.

Steinbier *(German: "stone beer")* 'smoky' German beer. Natural stone is heated on an open fire and dipped into the mash. The malt sugar caramelises on the surface of the stone. The stone is added again during lagering. See Rauchbier.

sterilise (to) to render something 100% free of germs.

stick (to) *(brewing)* to stop fermenting. If the fermentation temperature is too low, the fermentation may stick.

sticking *(brewing)* a term to describe a wort which has stopped fermenting prematurely.

Sticklebract a New Zealand general purpose hop with an alpha acid content of 11-12%.

stillage a brick, wooden or metal framework on which the casks are set up in the cellar. Also known as thralls or horsing.

stock ale traditionally a high-gravity beer matured for long periods (up to a year) in a vat or cask. Few today are commercially available in Britain.

stone square *(brewing)* a traditional form of fermenting vessel, square in shape and formerly made of stone or slate slabs. New ones tend to be stainless steel. The top is partially covered in, with a central hole to allow the escape of yeast and carbon dioxide. Originally more common in the north, but now dying out for economic reasons, they are often known as Yorkshire squares or slate squares.

Stonehenge Ale Wiltshire tower brewery, originally named Bunce's brewery after late founder Tony Bunco, housed in a listed building on the River Avon, established in 1984 and sold to Danish master brewer Stig Anker Andersen in 1993.

stoppered a bottle fitted with a stopper.

Storm Brewing Co. started brewing in 1998. Macclesfield based.

stout one of the classic types of ale, a successor in fashion to 'porter'. Usually a very dark, heavy, well-hopped bitter ale, with a dry palate, thick creamy head, and good grainy taste contributed by a proportion of dark roasted barley in the mash. Guinness is the best known bitter 'extra stout', of 1042 OG. The earliest uses of the word 'stout' indicate that it was applied to beers which were 'stout' in terms of strength; later, the word came to be associated with the idea of 'stout' in body, and was hence applied to the dark, full-bodied beer which was stronger and hoppier than porter. Ordinary stout in Ireland was comparable to 'plain porter'. See also Sweet Stout, Russian Stout.

stout lager Dutch bottom-fermented stouts.

strain a variety of yeast which shares specific characteristics e.g. flavouring properties.

straw *(beer evaluation)* a colour definition.

Strawberry Bank Brewery based at the rear of the Masons Arms pub in Cumbria. Arthur Ransome, the famous children's writer, lived up the lane next to the pub.

Streekbieren *(Flemish: "district beers")* Belgian speciality beers, which are associated uniquely with the locality where they are brewed.

strig the stalk of the hop cone.

strike heat *(brewing)* the temperature of the mash liquid before the grist is added.

strike temperature *(brewing)* the temperature of the water when the malt is added.

Strisselspalt a French aroma hop with an alpha acid content of 3-5%.

strobile the whole hop flower.

strong ale originally the partner of 'small beer'. The first wort run off the mash would produce what in Tudor times was referred to as 'doble' (double strength), a strong ale for men. The mash tun would be refilled with hot liquor, and the weaker second run-off of wort would be used to produce 'syngl' (single strength) or 'small beer' for women, children, and servants. Currently, any ale of over 1055 OG is generally regarded as a 'strong ale'.

stubby Australian slang for a small beer bottle.

style *(beer evaluation)* the sum of flavour and aroma by which individual beers can be categorised.

Styrian Goldings a Slovenian aroma hop with an alpha acid content of 4.5-5%. Also grown in US. Popular in Europe, especially UK.

sucre *(French)* sugar.

sugar *(brewing)* Brewers' sugar is an unrefined brown sugar, usually in block form. In many brews it is added to the wort at the copper boiling stage, increasing the fermentable material without requiring extra malt. Brewing sugars and syrups are known as copper sugars or copper syrups. In the past, landlords often added sugar to their casks in the pub cellar to re-ferment the beers to higher gravities. This illegal practice was so widespread that the licensing law carries a specific clause making it an offence for sugar to be found in a pub cellar.

suiker *(Dutch)* sugar.

Suk Korean rice beer.

sulphidic *(beer evaluation)* having a 'struck match' smell caused by sulphur dioxide produced by the yeast during fermentation.

sulphitic *(beer evaluation)* having a rotten egg smell caused by hydrogen sulphite, which is produced by the yeast during fermentation.

Sulwath Brewers Ltd. privately-owned Dumfries company that started brewing in 1995.

Summerskills Brewery Devon brewery set up in a vineyard near Kingsbridge in 1983, which in 1985 moved to Plymouth.

Sunset Cider & Wine Ltd. brewery situated under the The Leggers Inn pub in Dewsbury.

sunstruck *(beer evaluation)* a term to describe beer which has been over-exposed to bright lights resulting in the production of a 'skunky' aroma from the breakdown of hops. Also called light struck.

Super Pub a term for a trend in pub design: take out all the pub furniture to pack in as many young drinkers as possible, put in TV screens and pump up the volume. Super?

sur levure *(French)* with yeast sediment.

sur lie *(French)* with yeast sediment.

süß *(German)* sweet.

Sutton Brewing Co. brewery built alongside the Thistle Park Tavern, near Plymouth's Sutton Harbour.

svetle pivo *(Czech)* pale ale.

Swale Brewery established in 1995 in Sittingbourne, Kent.

Swale Brewery opened in 1995 in Milton Regis, Kent.

Swan Western Australia's major brewery, based in Perth. Besides Swan, it also produces Emu lager.

Swansea Brewing Company Swansea based brewery since 1996.

sweet *(beer evaluation)* having a sugary or honey aftertaste, caused by insufficient fermentation. Often described as "not fully attenuated."

sweet stout formerly called 'milk stout', until the Trade Descriptions Act ruled out the use of this terminology because the product does not contain milk. The 'milk' indicated that the stout's sweetness was derived from lactose.

sweet wort *(brewing)* the liquid that is run off from the mash tun into the copper prior to boiling. Sweet wort contains all of the fermentable sugars that have been extracted from the malt.

swifty *(slang)* a quick drink; also known as a swift one.

T-bar a tall pillar fount with several small name badges and switches arranged horizontally at the top.

table beer low alcohol sweet ale.

Taddy Ales beers from Sam Smith of Tadcaster, Yorkshire.

Tafelbier *(German; Flemish: "table beer")* sweet low alcohol pale or dark ale.

tail a pipe connector with a spigot.

takeover the act of assuming control or management of a company by another. CAMRA opposes all takeovers, which it believes lead to brewery closures and consequent reduction of consumer choice.

tall fount a tall pillar-tap mounting stationed on a bar, used to dispense the majority of traditional beers in Scotland. Beer is driven to the fount by air pressure or by electric pump. Term derives from 'fountain', but is pronounced 'font'. Founts were first used in Scotland in the 1830s. Common names include: Aitken, Grosvenor, McGlashan, Mackie & Carnegie.

Tally Ho a Devon hotel that has revived the 200-year-old tradition of brewing.

tank beer brewery-conditioned bright beer that is delivered in bulk by road tanker and then pumped into large tanks in the cellar of the pub or club. These tanks normally have a 90 or 180 gallon capacity. Tank beer is most common in the North of England, especially in the large social clubs.

tankard a large drinking vessel with a handle and sometimes a hinged lid. The diameter of the base is usually larger than that of the top.

tannin one of the chemicals extracted from the hops during the boiling in the copper; has both preservative and bittering properties.

tap an on-off tap that is driven into a traditional cask, through which the beer is drawn off. 'Tapping' is now often used as an expression for connection to any form of beer container, as in: 'This beer has only just been tapped' or 'I'll have to tap a new barrel'. Also part of a pub name, usually indicating a small basic pub that was an 'annexe' to a larger establishment e.g. brewery tap.

Tap n Tin Brew Pub Kent brewery established in 1999.

tap room basic public bar, traditionally where customers would sit alongside the stillaged casks of beer.

Target a disease-resistant British high-bittering copper hop, with an alpha acid content of 10-11%.

tarte à la bière a beer egg-custard dessert of Northern France.

tarwe *(Dutch/Flemish)* wheat.

tarwebier *(Dutch/Flemish)* wheat beer.

tarweboks Dutch wheat bock beers using a recipe with 30 per cent wheat.

tasting kit *(beer evaluation)* a set of standardised tastes and smells supplied to tasting panels so that different panels can describe beers using the same comparisons.

tasting panel *(beer evaluation)* a group of CAMRA members who are trained to taste beers according to strict criteria and taste comparisons. A tasting panel is able to detect changes in the taste of a beer following a move to a new brewery or a change of ingredients. The tasting notes from panels are included in the CAMRA Good Beer Guide.

tavern a hostelry historically catering for local custom, as opposed to an inn.

Taylor Walker London brewery taken over in 1960, with the name revived in 1980.

Ted and Ben a cask-conditioned organic beer brewed by Brakspear.

teetotaller a total abstainer from alcohol.

tegestologist a collector of beer mats.

Teignworthy Brewery established in 1994 by John and Rachel Lawton, brewing for outlets in Devon and Somerset.

Teme Valley Brewery Worcestershire inn that brews its own beer from its own hops.

Temperance Movement a major pressure group in the nineteenth century which initially promoted moderate drinking and then later espoused total abstinence.

tenant a licensee of a brewery-owned pub, held under a tenancy, as distinct from a salaried manager.

Tennent Caledonian Bass's Scottish company with breweries in Edinburgh and Glasgow. Best known for its lager, which has been brewed since 1885.

terminal gravity *(brewing)* final gravity.

Tetley Leeds brewery which merged with Ind Coope and Ansells in 1961 to form Allied Breweries. Thence it became half of Carlsberg-Tetley. Brewing since 1792, the Joshua Tetley Brewery is the biggest cask ale brewery in Britain. Famous for the tight creamy head on its beers and the Huntsman sign.

Tettnang a German aroma hop with an alpha acid content of 4-5%. Spicy aroma. Used for German-style beers.

Theakston famous Yorkshire Dales family brewers at Masham since 1827, who bought the former State brewery in Carlisle in 1974 to meet demand for their real ales. Renowned for their Old Peculier. Taken over by Matthew Brown of Blackburn in 1984.

thin *(beer evaluation)* pertaining to a lack of body.

thins *(malting)* rootlets and other waste shed by barley during the malting process.

Thomas McGuinness Brewing Co. Lancashire brewery since 1991.

Thorne Electrim *(homebrewing)* a purpose-built, polypropylene boiler.

thralls a brick, wooden or metal framework on which the casks are set up in the cellar. Also known as stillage or horsing.

Three Bs Brewery Blackburn brewery whose first beers went on sale in January 1999.

Three Inns Brewing Co Ltd. Shropshire brew pub.

Three Tuns historic homebrew pub at Bishop's Castle, Shropshire. The old brewery actually dwarfs the pub.

Thwaites traditional Blackburn brewery since excise officer Daniel started it up in 1807. Visitor centre and shop.

tie the means by which a brewery insists that a licensee sells their beers.

tied house a pub which is obliged to sell only the products of a particular brewery. CAMRA supports the relaxation of the tied house system without prejudicing the interests of local brewers. See Free House.

Tigertops Brewery Wakefield brewery established in 1995 by Stewart and Linda Johnson.

tight head the stiff creamy foam on top of the beer after it has been dispensed. A tight head is obtained by forcing the beer through very small orifices in the sparkler on the pump.

tight sparkler a device attached to the nozzle of the beer pump. The beer is forced through very small holes to aerate it and produce a creamy 'tight head'. The amount of aeration can be varied: screwed up for a creamy head or screwed out for a 'flat' pint. CAMRA is opposed to the growing tendency to serve southern-brewed beers with the aid of sparklers, which aerate the beer and tend to drive hop aroma and flavour into the head, altering the balance of the beer achieved in the brewery.

Timmermans one of Belgium's leading brewers of wild Lambic beers, from Itterbeek. Their bottled Gueuze is available in both 'naturelle' and filtered form.

Timothy Taylor & Co Ltd. Keighly family-owned brewery since 1858. The Knowle Spring brewery uses Pennines spring water.

Tindall Ales Brewery Bungay family brewery since 1998.

Tipsy Toad Brewery   Jersey brew pub launched by Steve Skinner in 1992 and taken over by Jersey Brewery in December 1997.

Tirril Brewery Cumbrian brew-inn taking the name of a brewery which closed in 1899.

Tisbury Brewery Ltd. Salisbury brewery which has retained name of brewery established in 1868.

Titanic Brewery Stoke-on-Trent brewery founded in 1985. Began brewing for demonstration purposes on the log-fired Victorian micro-brewery in the Staffordshire County Museum at Shugborough Hall.

tmave pivo *(Czech)* dark beer.

Toby Charrington's Toby Jug trademark – now usually inside a red triangle since becoming Bass Charrington in 1967 – which lends its name to a wide variety of Bass beers.

tocine pivo *(Czech)* draught beer.

toffee   *(beer evaluation)* having a treacly or cooked sugar flavour, often determined by the type of malt used.

Tollemache & Cobbold Brewery Ltd. Ipswich's Tolly Cobbold was founded by Thomas Cobbold in 1723. The site has now become a major tourist attraction.

Tom Hoskins Brewery PLC.   bought by Archers of Swindon in June 2000.

Tomintoul Brewery Co Ltd.   opened in Scotland in 1993 in an old water-mill.

Tomos Watkin Ltd. brewing in the Phoenix Brewery since 1995, now in the Swansea area.

Tooths   the Australian rival to Castlemaine-Tooheys in Sydney, best known for its Resch's KB lager.

top fermentation *(brewing)* fermentation in which the yeast rises to the top of the vessel in a thick foamy head. This is the method used for producing British ales, requiring a yeast of the Saccharomyces cerevisiae species. Top fermentation tends to be quite vigorous, generating considerable heat; a week or so is enough for most British brews.

top pressure the use of carbon dioxide under pressure to force beer up from the cellar to the counter fitting. Spoils the beer flavour by allowing too much gas to dissolve.

top-up   a request to a barman to fill the glass to the correct level so as to receive a full measure. In British law it is necessary to ask for a top-up and be refused, before proceeding with a complaint of short measure.

torrefied wheat   *(brewing)* adjunct used particularly in mild ales.

torrefy (to) to heat quickly at a high temperature.

Tower Bank Arms the rural inn in Cumbria, which appeared in an illustration by Beatrix Potter in her "Tale of Jemima Puddleduck".

tower brewery a 19th-century style of brewery, built as a tall narrow building. Arranged internally so that after the malt and water are raised to the uppermost floors, materials then flow downwards from process to process by gravity. Many such buildings are still readily identifiable although their original use has long since changed.

Townes Brewery Chesterfield based plant set up in 1994 in an old bakery.

traditional when applied to beer, 'traditional' has no definable meaning (as opposed to 'real ale' and 'cask conditioned'). If it is accepted that a practice continued for a generation (30 years) constitutes a tradition, then the brewing of lager in Wrexham and Alloa since the 1880s is 'traditional'. When applied to British breweries, 'traditional' implies that the processes of ale brewing are followed: e.g. use of the infusion mash tun rather than lauter tun or decoction systems, use of open fermenters, and no final processing (filtration, pasteurisation, recarbonation).

Trapistenbier *(German)* Trappist beer.

Trappist strong, top-fermenting, bottle-conditioned ales produced by the few surviving Trappist abbeys of Chimay, Orval, Rochefort, St Sixtus, and Westmalle in Belgium and Schaapskooi in the Netherlands.

Traquair House Brewery 18th-century brewhouse based in one of the wings of Scotland's oldest continually inhabited house in Peeblesshire (more than 1000 years old), where the Laird of Traquair recommenced brewing a rich dark ale in 1965 in 200 year old vessels.

Trimdon Cask Ales Co Durham brewery since 1999.

Tring Brewery Company Ltd. established in 1992 in Hertfordshire.

Tripel a term which refers to the former "xxx" branding on a cask. This was the former practice by breweries of branding their casks with a scale of crosses to denote the beer's strength, colour and maturation.

Tripel a very distinctive dark golden Trappist ale (8-9 per cent alcohol) produced by the Abbaye of Westmalle. The style has been copied by commercial Belgian and Dutch brewers using the Tripel name.

Triple fff Brewing Company Hampshire sole proprietorship since 1997.

trocken *(German)* dry.

trub *(brewing)* solid malt protein formed during boiling of the wort, which is removed prior to fermentation.

Truman former brewery in Brick Lane, reputably Britain's oldest brewery, dating back to 1666.

tube Australian slang for a can of beer.

Tuborg the internationally-known Danish brewery which, with Carlsberg, makes up United Breweries of Copenhagen.

tun *(brewing)* originally a very large oak cask of several hundred gallons but used now as a name for various brewery vessels, e.g. mash tun.

tut the small central piece of the shive.

Twelve Horse a strongish American ale (5 per cent alcohol) produced by Genesee of Rochester, New York.

Twentyfour Hours Festival an annual Belgian beer festival organised by Objectieve Bierproevers and held in Antwerp in September.

two-rowed barley barleycorns that grow in two-rowed ears, the most common variety found in the UK. Compare six-rowed barley.

U Fleku   famous Prague homebrew pub producing its own Czechoslovak dark lager.

Uley Brewery Ltd. G l o u c e s t e r s h i r e based, the Old Brewery has been housed since 1985 in what was formerly (since 1833), Price's Brewery.

ullage   the empty space between a liquid and the top of its container (bottle, cask etc.) Also called airspace; headspace.

ullage   waste beer, such as beer drawn off from pumps before serving, beer left in the cask, spillage, lees etc. CAMRA deplores the practice of returning waste beer to the cask and supports legislation to outlaw the use of waste beer. CAMRA believes that breweries should give fair ullage allowances to make this practice unnecessary.

umbrella *(brewing)* a structure within the copper that looks like a large mushroom. It operates rather like a coffee percolator: the boiling wort rises up the central column and cascades out over the domed top, thus ensuring very vigorous mixing of the copper's contents.

unaromatic *(beer evaluation)* without an aroma.

under licence when one brewery grants another, often abroad, permission to brew its recipe. Usually this results in an inferior product.

underage drinking illegal consumption of alcohol by those under the legal minimum age, which is 18 in the UK and 21 in USA. It is also an offence in UK for adults to supply under-18s with alcohol.

underback *(brewing)* a heated vessel that does some filtering and is also often used to dissolve any brewers' sugar that is to be added to the brew. When the mash is complete the wort, containing the dissolved malt sugars, is run off into the copper. This run-off is via the underback.

underletting *(brewing)* when hot water is run into the base of the mash tun, beneath the false bottom, to increase the temperature of the mash and to lift the mash off the plates to improve run off.

Union   Burton Union: a traditional open fermentation method, during which the beer rises out of large oak casks through swan-neck pipes into long troughs for use in pitching into following brews. It is this system which made Draught Bass famous, but they closed their Union rooms in the early 1980s. The future of Burton Union open fermenters is uncertain following a Health & Safety Executive ruling which states that open fermenters must be covered to exclude all carbon dioxide from the fermenting room.

unit of alcohol 8 grammes of alcohol. A half pint of ordinary strength beer or lager (3% alcohol) is equivalent to one unit. A half pint of strong beer or lager (5.5% alcohol) is equivalent to two units. Up to 21 units of alcohol per week for men and up to 14 units of alcohol per week for women are generally considered by the medical profession to be within safe limits of alcohol consumption.

United Breweries the giant company of Denmark which includes Carlsberg and Tuborg, and is linked with the Rupert Group of South Africa.

untergärig *(German)* bottom-fermented.

ur *(German: "original")*. Sometimes also Urtyp. Term adopted only by breweries which created a beer style (e.g. Spaten Ur-Märzen or Pilsner Urquell).

Ushers Brewery Ltd. West Country brewery, founded in 1824 by Thomas Usher but closed in 2000. Some of the Usher's beers were transferred to the Thomas Hardy Brewery in Dorchester.

Vale Brewery Company
Buckinghamshire brewery run by two brothers.

Valhalla Brewery brewing since 1997 on the island of Unst in the Shetland Isles, making it the most northerly brewery in Great Britain.

van 't vat *(Dutch)* on draught.

vat *(traditional; brewing)* a large tank in a brewery, more usually an open one such as a fermenting vessel. Tank is the term more usually applied in a big commercial brewery.

vault North of England alternative to the Public Bar; originally the room where the casks were stored.

Vaux Northeast brewing group, closed – despite remaining profitable and providing valuable jobs – by city analysts.

Veltins a German brewery in the Ruhrgebiet.

venting the release of excess carbon dioxide built up in a cask during secondary fermentation. The gas is released slowly via a soft spile. See spile.

venting peg alternative term for a spile.

Ventnor Brewery Ltd. Isle of Wight brewer since the early 1840s, using St. Boniface natural spring water.

Ventonwyn Brewing Company
new brewery, named after a local Cornish tin mine.

verre *(French)* glass.

verticillium wilt a disease affecting hops which has led to the development of wilt-resistant varieties like Target.

Verulam Brewery brewery housed behind the Farmer's Boy pub in St Albans, Hertfordshire.

vessel a container for liquids.

Victoriana a style of decor much loved by modern interior designers, intended to recall the days of the Gin Palace, characterised by dark timber, mirrors, and pseudo-gas lamps. Sometimes achieved at great expense in pubs whose original Victorian features were ripped out a decade previously.

victualler traditionally a purveyor of food. Hence, licensed victualler should refer to a purveyor of food and alcoholic beverages.

Vienna a strong copper-coloured lager style created in Austria's capital, but popularised over the border in Germany where it is known as Märzen.

Vienna malt malt which gives a distinctive malt and nutty character to the brew. Often used for Märzenbier and stronger lagers. EBC: 7-15.

village pub a house in an out-of-town location, open to the public at stated times for the purpose of social drinking. CAMRA believes that village pubs are essential community amenities and should be eligible to receive 50% mandatory relief on their business rates.

vintage beers not only does wine improve with age; so do a few beers, notably strong Belgian bottle-conditioned ales. Blue-capped Chimay is best after two years but can be kept for five. Liefmans Provisie also reaches a peak after two years but matures for another 25. In Britain, Courage year-dates its Imperial Russian Stout and Eldridge Pope recommend their Thomas Hardy Ale be kept for five years.

viscosity   the body.

volatiles   beer volatiles: esters, aldehydes, higher alcohols and other organic chemicals, which all affect the flavour of the beer (for better or worse). They are the by-products of fermentation and can be controlled by correct fermentation procedures and adjuncts.

Vollbier   *(German: "full beer")* a category of beer in Germany which includes all medium strength beers with between 4.4 and 5.65% abv.

vollmundig *(German: "full-mouthed")* full-bodied.

vom Fass (or Faß) *(German)*   on draught.

Wadworth & Co Ltd.   N o r t h g a t e Brewery set up by Henry Wadworth. Its mighty dray horses have dominated the market town of Devizes since 1885. Probably best known for its 6X in the free trade.

Walker   Peter Walker subsidiary of Tetley Walker, formed in 1981 to run 76 highly traditional pubs, mainly on Merseyside.

wallop   *(slang)* mild ale.

Wanderhausen   from the German 'wandering house'; a modern malting system deploying huge moving trays, an adaptation of the Saladin box system.

Warcop Country Ales   Gwent brewery based in a converted milking parlour.

Wards   former Sheffield brewery, that became part of the Vaux Group in 1972 and closed in 2000.

Warwickshire Beer Co. Ltd.   b r e w - ery based in a former village bakery.

wassail   the old English name for a festive drinking session and formerly an Anglo-Saxon toast made to a person at such a festivity: 'Ves heill' means 'be in good health'.

Wasser   *(German)* water.

waste beer   beer drawn off from pumps before serving, beer left in the cask, spillage, lees etc. CAMRA deplores the practice of returning waste beer to the cask and supports legislation to outlaw the use of waste beer.

water   *(brewing)* liquor.

water engine   a machine mounted on pub cellar walls that converts ordinary mains water pressure into compressed air for use in air-pressure beer dispense, using a series of slide valves. Only a few engines remain in active use, in Scotland.

water filter   *(homebrewing)* a tap attachment which will remove chlorine and other undesirable heavy metals from the water supply

water hardness   the level of minerals in the water supply.

water treatment   the removal of excessive carbonates from the water supply and the addition of sulphates: a fine balance to ensure the correct pH value of the mash. See Burtonising.

Wawne Brewery   Yorkshire brewery set up in April 1999 by home-brew enthusiast Mike Gadie in his garage.

wee heavy   Scottish term for a nip-sized bottle of strong ale. Name first used for Fowler's Wee Heavy, the famous 1110 OG brew of John Fowler of Prestonpans, East Lothian.

Wee Willie   Younger's bottled brown and pale ales (1032). Name chiefly used in Northern Ireland.

Weetwood Ales Ltd. Cheshire brewery set up at an equestrian centre in 1993.

Weihenstephan Bavarian brewery at Freising, north of Munich, reputedly the oldest in the world, dating back to 1040. Now linked with the state-owned Hofbrauhaus, it cooperates with Bavaria's institute of brewing, notably to produce Weizen (wheat) beers.

Weißbier *(German)* white beer made from wheat malt instead of barley malt. Also called Weizen.

Weisse *(German)* white beer. The term usually refers to the top-fermented pale brews of Berlin (see Berliner Weisse.) Similar beers are produced elsewhere in Germany, and also to the east of Brussels in the village of Hoegaarden.

Weizen *(German: "wheat")* wheat beer originating from South Germany (Bavaria), using much more wheat in the mash than the Weisse (white) beers of Berlin. They are also stronger and come in a variety of styles from Hefeweizen (with sediment) and filtered Hefefrei (yeast-free) to strong Weizenbocks, some bottom-fermented, others top. Notable Weizen brewers are Hofbrauhaus, Sanwald, and Weihenstephan. Weizen beer glasses are very tall. They are narrow at the bottom and have a bulb at the top.

Weizenbock *(German)* Bockbier, brewed using wheat malt. Depending on the type of malt used you can have dunkles Weizenbock (dark) and helles Weizenbock (light).

Wells see Charles Wells.

Welsh Brewers this was Bass's Welsh company with 500 pubs and a brewery in Cardiff, and is now Brains, following the brewery's sale in 1999. Formerly Hancock's Brewery.

Weltons North Downs Brewery Ltd. installed in a renovated milking parlour near Dorking in 1995 but now in a factory unit.

Wentworth Brewery Ltd. brewing in Yorkshire since 1999, using old Stones and Wards equipment.

West Berkshire Brewery Co. Ltd. established in 1995 by Dave and Helen Maggs in converted farm buildings in the grounds of the Pot Kiln pub.

West Yorkshire Brewery Halifax based, formerly the Black Horse Brewery.

Westmalle Abbaye on the Dutch border, producing the most unusual Belgian Trappist beer, Tripel. There is also a darker 'double'.

wet rent the traditional method of renting a pub to a tenant: the building was rented for a very low, almost nominal, sum and then most of the brewery's income was by way of a surcharge on the wholesale price of the drink – the wet rent. This has now largely given way to very much higher rents on the property.

Wethered formerly Whitbread's Buckinghamshire brewery at Marlow.

WH Brakspear & Sons plc. brewery based on an historic site in Henley upon Thames. The 19th century brewhouse and Tun Room still incorporate the unique two-tier dropping system of fermentation.

What's Brewing monthly newspaper, free to CAMRA members.

Wheal Ale Brewery Ltd. Cornish brewery founded in 1980 as Parkside Brewery. Based at the Bird in Hand pub in Hayle.

Wheat Bok a Dutch specialist beer style first produced in 1992 using 30 per cent wheat. Known as Tarwebock.

wheat flakes *(brewing)* a cereal used as an adjunct, chiefly in mild ales.

wheat flour *(brewing)* an unmalted adjunct used to improve head retention and to dilute the nitrogen in malt.

wheat malt light-coloured malt used to improve head retention and also the predominant malt in wheat beers. EBC: 3.5-5.

Whim Ales Derbyshire brewery since 1993.

whirlpool *(brewing)* a separation vessel which clarifies the wort by injecting it tangentially into the vessel. The resultant spin separates out solids to the centre of the vessel where it forms a cone. The clear wort is run off from the side of the vessel leaving the cone intact. Compare: centrifuge.

Whitbread national brewer which heavily rationalised its breweries from the early 1980s until finally getting out of brewing completely. The company continued to develop branded pub chains, only to sell them and turn itself into a property/hotel business.

Whitbread Archive organised collection of records since 1750 from Whitbread and the many companies with which it has been associated.

Whitbread Golding a British aroma hop with an alpha acid content of 7-8%.

White ale an old West Country medicinal concoction combining beer, rum, eggs, flour and a pinch of salt.

white beer unfiltered wheat beer with a 'milky' protein haze. See Weisse.

White Brewing Company operates at The 1066 Country Brewery in East Sussex. Founded in May 1995.

White lambic   a beer style which combines old lambic with young wheat beer. Fruit essence may be added.

white malt lightly kilned malted barley, with a pale colour (5 EBC).

Whitewater Brewing Co. Northern Ireland brewery founded in 1996 on a farm outside Kilkeel.

Wicked Hathern Brewery Ltd. Loughborough brewery opened in 2000.

Wickwar Brewing Co. Gloucestershire brewery launched in 1990.

Wiener   a lager (4.5-5.5% abv) using a dark, rich malt from Wien (Vienna).

Wieze Oktoberfesten annual beer festival in Belgium held from the end of September to mid October.

wild beer a beer style unique to Belgium, produced by spontaneous fermentation. Wild yeasts from the air ferment these wheat brews from the Senne Valley, west of Brussels, giving them a unique sour taste and an alcohol content of 4.5 per cent. See lambic.

Wilde Kersen Bier beer flavoured with wild cherries from Van Honsebrouck's Terschelling. See Kriek.

Willamette an American aroma hop variety with a 4.5-5.5% alpha acid content, which imparts a spicy, grassy, floral aroma.

William Younger Scottish & Newcastle's southern England and South Wales marketing company.

Willy's Brewery Ltd. Cleethorpes brewery opened in 1989 to provide beer for two outlets in Grimsby and Cleethorpes.

Wilson Watney's Manchester brewery.

wilt a disease (full name verticillium wilt) affecting hops which has led to the development of wilt-resistant varieties like Target.

Winchester Ale Houses Ltd. a group of pubs brewing for their own consumption.

Winfields Brewery Hampshire pub brewery set up in 1995.

Winkles small North Derbyshire brewery set up in a former bomb factory in Buxton in 1979, now concentrating on its family chain of tied houses.

Winston a strong Belgian beer (7.5 per cent alcohol).

winter ale now virtually synonymous with 'old ale'. Most 'winter ales' are produced and sold for a limited period in the year, usually between November and the end of February. Usually a rich, dark, malty high-gravity draught ale of considerable body. Such ales feature prominently at CAMRA's Winter Beer Festival.

witbier   *(Dutch)* white beer.

Wolf Brewery Ltd. Norfolk brewery founded in 1996 by the former owner of the Reindeer Brewery.

Wood Brewery Ltd. S h r o p s h i r e brewery started in 1980. Sam Powell Brewery and its beers were acquired in 1991.

Woodbury Brewery Worcestershire brewery set up in 1997 in a stable block.

Woodfordes Norfolk Ales brewing company which has brewed at the Broadland Brewery, Woodbastwick since 1989. Founded in 1981 in Drayton near Norwich.

Woodhampton Brewing Co. Herefordshire brewery since May 1997.

Worcester Goldings a British aroma hop with an alpha acid content of 4.5-6.5%.

Worfield Brewing Co. Ltd. Shropshire brewery set up in 1994 at the Davenport Arms.

work (to) *(brewing)* to ferment.

Worldham Brewery Hampshire brewery in an old oast house.

wort *(brewing)* the sweet liquid, containing all the extracts from the malted grain, which subsequently will be fermented into beer. The extract run off from the mash tun is the sweet wort; after boiling with the hops it is the hopped wort.

wort boiler *(brewing)* the brew kettle.

wort chiller homebrewing equipment to cool the wort quickly.

wort cooler *(brewing)* a cooling vessel for the wort once the hops have been strained.

wort copper *(brewing)* a brew kettle.

wort kettle *(brewing)* a brew kettle.

wort receiver *(brewing)* a wort holding tank.

wort straining *(brewing)* the process of filtering or sieving the wort.

Worthington Burton brewer who merged with Bass in 1927. The brewery has since been demolished but the name survives on various beers.

worting *(traditional; brewing)* the adding of wort as a priming sugar to a cask.

wowser Australian slang for a non-drinker or killjoy.

Wrexham the oldest lager brewery in Britain, founded in 1882 and taken over by Ind Coope in 1949. Still brews Wrexham Lager for North Wales, although now specialises in brewing foreign lagers under licence.

würzig *(German: "strong-tasting")* full-bodied.

Wychwood Brewery Co. Ltd. set up as Glenny Brewery in 1983, in the old maltings of the extinct Clinch's brewery, Wychwood moved to a new site in 1987 and was radically revamped during 1992.

Wye Valley Brewery Ltd.
Herefordshire brewery in rear of pub, launched in 1985.

Wyeast   a range of liquid yeasts from America.

Wyre Piddle Brewery   Worcestershire brewery established in 1992.

X   a mark by 17th-century excisemen used to denote the single- (X) or double-strength (XX) wort (see strong ale). The practice spread; its original purpose was lost, and it became a (dubious) claim of strength and quality, with brewers marking their casks XXX, XXXX, or even XXXXXX. The number of Xs today does not indicate any regular measure of strength.

yard of ale   a long, glass vessel (holding between 2 1/4 and 4 1/2 pints), used for drinking contests, with a surprise for the unwary in its bulbous end. If it is tilted too sharply, beer will flood over the drinker's face. A possible forerunner might have been the Viking drinking horn.

Yard of Flannel   a yard of mild, flavoured with Cognac, sugar and spices and mixed with beaten eggs.

Yates Brewery   started in Cumbria in 1986. Now supplies Lake District, Tyneside and Wearside pubs.

yeast a microscopic (normally) single-celled fungus of the genus Ascomycetes able to metabolise carbohydrate. The waste products excreted include alcohol and carbon dioxide together with many more complex organic chemicals. Yeasts come in many strains and, while all produce alcohol, the mix of the other chemicals varies so that different yeasts produce different flavours. In the past, brewers just kept yeast from one brew to start the next, and so on indefinitely; as most of the yeasts are mixtures of different strains, and the mixtures can change with time, this can give rise to changes in the resulting beer. It is now common practice to propagate single strains from one selected cell. These yeasts may be used for a number of brews and then a new batch will be propagated to keep the strain pure. To satisfy CAMRA's definition of a pure beer, there should be no substantial removal of yeast at any time during the brewing process, unless reseeding is practised. Pure beer must contain at least 0.5 million live cells/ml after racking into cask.

yeast back *(brewing)* a vessel to hold yeast before re-pitching.

yeast bite *(beer evaluation)* a sour, harshly bitter taste.

yeast food   yeast nutrients.

yeast frets *(brewing)* an obvious secondary fermentation in the cask. Can be caused by wild yeast.

yeast head *(brewing)* the froth at the surface of top-fermenting ale at the end of primary fermentation.

yeast nutrients the essential life substances of yeast cells which include oxygen, nitrogenous material, minerals and vitamins.

yeasting *(brewing)* pitching: to add yeast into the fermenting vessel. After the malted grain is mashed and the liquid (wort) is run off into fermenting vessels, the fermentation is started by the addition of yeast.

yeasty *(beer evaluation)* having a yeast-like aftertaste and aroma.

Yella Belly a cask-conditioned organic beer brewed by Bateman's.

Yeoman a high-bittering copper hop with an alpha acid content of 10.6.

York Brewery Company Ltd. producing since 1996, this show brewery has a visitor centre, gift shop and bar.

Yorkshire name given to keg and cask bitters from the county when sold in the south, notably John Smith's and Webster's.

Yorkshire square *(brewing)* a traditional form of fermenting vessel, square in shape and formerly made of stone or slate slabs. New ones tend to be stainless steel. The top is partially covered in, with a central hole to allow the escape of yeast and carbon dioxide. Originally more common in the north, but now dying out for economic reasons. They are also known as squares.

Young & Co's Brewery PLC London's famous independent family brewers who stood alone against the keg tide in the Capital in the early 1970s. Young's has brewed at the Earn Brewery in Wandsworth continuously since 1581, making it the oldest site in Britain.

Younger an old brewing name subsumed into the Scottish Courage plc.

Yuengling the oldest brewery in the United States, in Pottsville, Pennsylvania, dating back to 1829, and known for its 'celebrated' Pottsville Porter.

Zambezi   a South African lager from the National Breweries, Zimbabwe.

Zenith   high-bittering copper hop with an alpha acid content of 9.0.

Zomerboks *(Dutch)*   Summer bock beers.

zonder scheikundige Produkten *(Flemish)* without chemical additives.

Zucker   *(German)* sugar.

Zum Uerige famous old homebrew house in Düsseldorf, Germany, producing the unique German dark ale, Alt.

zymamonas *(brewing)* an anaerobic bacterium, whose action produces slimy gelatinous threads in beer. A cask can be completely ruined in a matter of hours. Easily controlled by scrupulous hygiene as well as clean casks and efficient cask washers.

zymase   a mixture of enzymes extracted from yeast which causes the alcoholic fermentation of sugars.

zymologist a person working in the field of zymology.

zymology the chemistry or study of fermentation.

zymolysis the process of fermentation.

zymometer an instrument for measuring the degree of fermentation.

zymosis   the process of fermentation. Another name for zymolysis.

zymotechnics the science of fermentation.

zymotic   relating to fermentation.

zymurgy the art and science of brewing. Also the name of an American homebrewers' magazine.

Zythos   *(Greek)* a barley wine.

CAMRA Books

The CAMRA Books range of guides helps you search out the best in beer (and cider) and brew it at home too!

Buying in the UK

All our books are available through bookshops in the UK. If you can't find a book, simply order it from your bookshop using the ISBN number, title and author details given below. CAMRA members should refer to their regular monthly newspaper What's Brewing for the latest details and member special offers. CAMRA books are also available by mail-order (postage free) from: CAMRA Books, 230 Hatfield Road, St Albans, Herts, AL1 4LW. Cheques made payable to CAMRA Ltd. Telephone your credit card order on 01727 867201.

Buying outside the UK

CAMRA books are also sold in many book and beer outlets in the USA and other English-speaking countries. If you have trouble locating a particular book, use the details below to order with your credit card (or US$ cheque) by mail, email (info@camra. org. uk), fax (+44 1727 867670) or web site. The web site (www. camra. org. uk) will securely process credit card purchases.

Carriage of £3.00 per book (Europe) and £6.00 per book (US, Australia, New Zealand and other overseas) is charged.

UK Booksellers

Call CAMRA Books for distribution details and book list. CAMRA Books are listed on all major CD-ROM book lists and on our Internet site: http://www. camra. org. uk

Overseas Booksellers

Call or fax CAMRA Books for details of local distributors.

Distributors are required for some English language territories and rights are available for electronic and non-English language editions. Enquiries should be addressed to the managing editor (mark-webb@msn. com).

CAMRA Guides

Painstakingly researched and checked, these guides are the leaders in their field, bringing you to the door of pubs which serve real ale and more...

CAMRA's London Pubs Guide

by Lynne Pearce

256 pages   Price: £9.99

This is the guide to CAMRA's favourite London pubs, chosen because these pubs sell traditional real ale, often brewed in the capital itself. The guide also points out the pub features you will want to discover on your trip around London: the architecture, personalities, history, local ambience and nearby attractions.

Practical aids to getting you to the pub(s) of your choice include transportation details and street level maps. Each entry also provides information about opening times, travel details, food arrangements, parking, disabled and children's facilities. Plus the all-important range of beers.

Feature articles in the book include a history of brewing in London and a guide to London's best pub food. Real ale and great food in London pubs with stories to tell. What could be better?

Use the following code to order this book from your bookshop: ISBN 1-85249-164-7

CAMRA's Good Cider Guide

by David Matthews

400 pages   Price: £9.99

CAMRA's guide to real cider researched anew for the new Millennium and now with features on cider around the world – North America, France, Spain.

The guide contains three main sections:

Features on cider-making from around the world, bottled cider and cider traditions.

⌣   A comprehensive and detailed guide to UK producers of cider. Each producer entry includes details of the ciders produced, availability, cost, and visitor information. There are also notes on the producer's cider-making background and history. All this data is newly surveyed by the editor and a huge team of CAMRA volunteers.

⌣   A brand new listing of outlets – pubs, restaurants, bars, small cider makers – with full address including postcode and telephone contact numbers. Details of ciders available and, where appropriate, items of interest in the pub or area.

Use the following code to order this book from your bookshop: ISBN 1-85249-143-4

Room at the Inn 2nd edition

by Jill Adam

324 pages   Price: £8.99

This second edition of the hugely popular *Room at the Inn* is your guide to quality overnight accommodation with a decent selection of real ale for good measure. The guide has been completely resurveyed and researched from scratch by the grass roots experts of the Campaign for Real Ale. Each entry in the guide gives local directions, contact details, opening times, type and extent of accommodation, list of beers, meal types and times, easy to understand price guide and snippets about local attractions and the sometimes centuries-old tales associated with your resting place.

Use the following code to order this book from your bookshop: ISBN 1-85249-150-7

Heritage Pubs of Great Britain

by Mark Bolton and James Belsey

144 pages hard back   Price: £16.99

It is still possible to enjoy real ale in sight of great craftsmanship and skill. What finer legacy for today's drinkers? Feast your eyes and toast the architects and builders from times past. This full colour collectible is a photographic record of some of the finest pub interiors in Britain. Many of the pubs included have been chosen from CAMRA's national inventory of pub interiors which should be saved at all costs. As a collector's item, it is presented on heavy, gloss-art paper in a sleeved hard back format. The pub interiors have been photographed by architectural specialist Mark Bolton and described in words by pub expert James Belsey.

Available only from CAMRA – call 01727 867201 (overseas +44 1727 867201)

Pubs for Families

by David Perrott

308 pages   Price: £8.99

Traditional pubs with CAMRA-approved ale and a warm welcome for the kids! Nothing could be better. But where to find such a hospitable hostel on home patch, let alone when out and about or on holiday? *Pubs for Families* contains invaluable national coverage with easy to use symbols so that you know what facilities are available and regional maps so you'll know how to get there. Get the best of both worlds with this invaluable guide.

Use the following code to order this book from your bookshop: ISBN 1-85249-141-8

Good Pub Food 5th edition

by Susan Nowak

448 pages approx   Price: £9.99

The pubs in these pages serve food as original and exciting as anything available in far more expensive restaurants. And, as well as the exotic and unusual, you will find landlords and land-ladies serving simple, nourishing pub fare such as a genuine ploughman's lunch or a steak and kidney pudding.

Award-winning food and beer writer Susan Nowak, who has travelled the country to complete this fifth edition of the guide, says that 'eating out' started in British inns and taverns and this guide is a contribution to an appreciation of all that is best in British food…and real cask-conditioned ale.

Use the following code to order this book from your bookshop: ISBN 1-85249-151-5

50 Great Pub Crawls

by Barrie Pepper

256 pages   Price: £9.99

Visit the beer trails of the UK, from town centre walks, to hikes and bikes and a crawl on a train on which the pubs are even situated on your side of the track!

Barrie Pepper, with contributions and recommendations from CAMRA branches, has compiled a 'must do' list of pub crawls, with easy to use colour maps to guide you, notes on architecture, history and brewing tradition to entertain you.

Use the following code to order this book from your bookshop: ISBN 1-85249-142-6

Good Beer Guides

These are comprehensive guides researched by professional beer writers and CAMRA enthusiasts. Use these guides to find the best beer on your travels or to plan your itinerary for the finest drinking. Travel and accommodation information, plus maps, help you on your way and there's plenty to read about the history of brewing, the beer styles and the local cuisine to back up the entries for bars and beverages.

Good Beer Guide to Belgium, Holland and Luxembourg

by Tim Webb

286 pages   Price: £9.99

Discover the stunning range and variety of beers available in the Low Countries, our even nearer neighbours via Le Tunnel. Channel-hopping Tim Webb's latest edition – the third – of the guide offers even more bars in which an incredible array of beers can be enjoyed. There are maps, tasting notes, beer style guide and a beers index to complete the most comprehensive companion to drinking with your Belgian and Dutch hosts.

Use the following code to order this book from your bookshop: ISBN 1-85249-139-6

Good Beer Guide to Northern France

by Arthur Taylor

256 pages   Price: £7.99

Discover the excitement of the bars and cafes, the tranquillity of the village breweries which hold the secrets of generations of traditional brewing. Join the many festivals and cultural events such as the beer-refreshed second-hand market in Lille and the presentation of the Christmas ales. Find out where the best beer meets the best mussels and chips. Cuisine à la bière and more! Arthur Taylor is a leading authority on French beer and a member of Les Amis de la Bière, who have co-operated in the research for this book.

Use the following code to order this book from your bookshop: ISBN 1-85249-140-X

Good Bottled Beer Guide

by Jeff Evans

128 pages+   Price: £8.99

Now in its third edition, *Good Bottled Beer Guide* is becoming the complete guide to buying bottle-conditioned beers, including features on the main ingredients and identifying the flavours. When early nights and unfriendly traffic conspire to keep you at home, there's no risk these days of missing out on drinking a fine real ale. Britain's off-licences and supermarkets now stock bottle-conditioned ales – real ale in a bottle. The book lists all known bottle-conditioned beers and gives ingredients and tasting notes, plus contact information for out of the way producers.

Use the following code to order this book from your bookshop: ISBN 1-85249-173-6

Good Beer Guide

edited by Roger Protz

750 pages approx   Price: £12.99

Produced annually in early October

Fancy a pint? Let CAMRA's Good Beer Guide lead the way. Revised each year to include around 5,000 great pubs serving excellent ale -- country pubs, town pubs and pubs by the sea.

Fully and freshly researched by members of the Campaign for Real Ale, real enthusiasts who use the pubs week in, week out. No payment is ever taken for inclusion. The guide has location maps for each county and you can read full details of all Britain's breweries (big and small) and the ales they produce, including tasting notes.

Other Books

Cellarmanship

by Ivor Clissold

144 pages   Price: £6.99

This book explains every aspect of running a good cellar and serving a great pint of real ale which does both pub and brewer proud. It's a must have book for all professionals in the drinks trade, for all those studying at college to join it, and for all those who need to tap a cask of real ale for a party or beer festival.

Use the following code to order this book from your bookshop: ISBN 1-85249-126-4

Brewery Breaks

by Ted Bruning

64 pages   Price: £3.99

A handy pocket guide to brewery visitor centres and museums. Keep this in the car on your travels and you'll never be far from the living history of brewing. An ideal reference for CAMRA members, and others, wishing to organise a trip to one of Britain's best known breweries or a tasting at a local microbrewery.

Use the following code to order this book from your bookshop: ISBN 1-1-85249-132-9

CAMRA Quiz Book

by Jeff Evans

128 pages   Price: £3.99

Fun and games for beer fans, and their relations. Use this book to quiz your mates on real ale and CAMRA history. Great for fund-raising quiz events and for catching up on the campaign.

Use the following code to order this book from your bookshop: ISBN 1-85249-127-2

Kegbuster Cartoon Book

by Bill Tidy

72 pages, including colour cartoons   Price: £4.99

A classic, hilarious, collection of cartoons from well-known funny man and cartoonist extraordinaire Bill Tidy. The perfect gift for the beer lover in your life!

Use the following code to order this book from your bookshop: ISBN 1-1-85249-134-5

Brew Your Own

Learn the basics of brewing real ales at home from the experts. And then move on to more ambitious recipes which imitate well-loved ales from the UK and Europe.

Homebrew Classics – Indian Pale Ale

by Clive La Pensée and Roger Protz

Pages: 196 pages   Price: £8.99

The Homebrew Classics series tells you everything you need to know about particular beer styles. Indian Pale Ale provides the background knowledge about ingredients and technique so that you can can reproduce the style authentically with your homebrew equipment.

In order to create this series CAMRA has brought together the talents of home brewer Clive La Pensée and beer journalist Roger Protz. La Pensée brings the practical and technical knowhow and Protz delivers the knowledge of beer styles – their history, provenance and modern ingredients as commercially brewed.

The result is a collection of recipes which allow the home brewer to replicate the famous IPA style of cask-conditioned beer. Look out for the other titles in the series: Mild, Stout & Porter, Bitter and more.

Use the following code to order this book from your bookshop: ISBN: 1-85249-129-9

Brew your own Real Ale at Home

by Graham Wheeler and Roger Protz

194 pages   Price: £8.99

This book contains recipes which allow you to replicate some famous cask-conditioned beers at home or to customise brews to your own particular taste. Conversion details are given so that the measurements can be used world-wide.

Use the following code to order this book from your bookshop: ISBN 1-85249-138-8

Brew Classic European Beers at Home

by Graham Wheeler and Roger Protz

196 pages   Price: £8.99

Keen home brewers can now recreate some of the world's classic beers. In your own home you can brew superb pale ales, milds, porters, stouts, Pilsners, Alt, Kolsch, Trappist, wheat beers, sour beers, even the astonishing fruit lambics of Belgium… and many more. Measurements are given in UK, US and European units, emphasising the truly international scope of the beer styles within.

Use the following code to order this book from your bookshop: ISBN 1-85249-117-5

Home Brewing

by Graham Wheeler

240 pages   Price: £8.99

Recently redesigned to make it even easier to use, this is the classic first book for all home-brewers. While being truly comprehensive, Home Brewing also manages to be a practical guide which can be followed step by step as you try your first brews. Plenty of recipes for beginners and hints and tips from the world's most revered home brewer.

Use the following code to order this book from your bookshop: ISBN 1-85249-137-X

JOIN CAMRA

If you like good beer and good pubs you could be helping to fight to preserve, protect and promote them. CAMRA was set up in the early seventies to fight against the mass destruction of a part of Britain's heritage. The giant brewers are still pushing through takeovers, mergers and closures of their smaller regional rivals. They are still trying to impose national brands of beer and lager on their customers whether they like it or not, and they are still closing down town and village pubs or converting them into grotesque 'theme' pubs.

CAMRA wants to see genuine free competition in the brewing industry, fair prices, and, above all, a top quality product brewed by local breweries in accordance with local tastes, and served in pubs that maintain the best features of a tradition that goes back centuries.

As a CAMRA member you will be able to enjoy generous discounts on CAMRA products and receive the highly rated monthly newspaper *What's Brewing*. You will be given the CAMRA members' handbook and be able to join in local social events and brewery trips.

To join, complete the form below and, if you wish, arrange for direct debit payments by filling in the form overleaf and returning it to CAMRA. To pay by credit card, contact the membership secretary on (01727) 867201.

Full membership £14; Joint (living partners') membership £17; Single under 26 £8; Joint under 26 membership £11; retired over 60, student, unemployed £8; Joint retired over 60 £11; UK/EU Life membership £168   Please delete as appropriate: I/We wish to become members of CAMRA.   I/We agree to abide by the memorandum and articles of association of the company.   I/We enclose a cheque/p. o. for £   (payable to CAMRA Ltd.)
Name(s)
Address
Postcode
Signature(s)
CAMRA Ltd. , 230 Hatfield Road, St Albans, Herts AL1 4LW

Instruction to your Bank or Building Society to pay by Direct Debit

Please fill in the whole form using a ball point pen and send it to:

Campaign for Real Ale Ltd,
230 Hatfield Road,
St. Albans,
Herts
AL1 4LW

Name of Account Holder(s)

Bank/Building Society account number

Branch Sort Code

Name and full postal address of your Bank or Building Society

To The Manager	Bank/Building Society
Address	
	Postcode

Originator's Identification Number

| 9 | 2 | 6 | 1 | 2 | 9 |

Reference Number

FOR CAMRA OFFICIAL USE ONLY
This is not part of the instruction to your Bank or Building Society

Membership Number

Name

Postcode

Instructions to your Bank or Building Society
Please pay CAMRA Direct Debits from the account detailed on this instruction subject to the safeguards assured by the Direct Debit Guarantee. I understand that this instruction may remain with CAMRA and, if so, will be passed electronically to my Bank/Building Society

Signature(s)

Date

Banks and Building Societies may not accept Direct Debit instructions for some types of account

✂ -

This guarantee should be detached and retained by the Payer.

The Direct Debit Guarantee

■ This Guarantee is offered by all Banks and Building Societies that take part in the Direct Debit Scheme. The efficiency and security of the Scheme is monited and protected by your own Bank or Building Society.

■ If the amounts to be paid or the payment dates change CAMRA will notify you 10 working days in advance of your account being debited or as otherwise agreed.

■ If an error is made by CAMRA or your Bank or Building Society, you are guaranteed a full and immediate refund from your branch of the amount paid.

■ You can cancel a Direct Debit at any time by writing to your Bank or Building Society. Please also